STREAMS

their dynamics and
morphology

EARTH AND PLANETARY SCIENCE SERIES

PATRICK M. HURLEY, *Consulting Editor*

AHRENS   Distribution of the Elements in Our Planet
FAUL   Ages of Rocks, Planets, and Stars
MORISAWA   Streams: Their Dynamics and Morphology
WOOD   Meteorites and the Origin of Planets

STREAMS
their dynamics and morphology

Marie Morisawa

ANTIOCH COLLEGE

McGraw-Hill Book Company

NEW YORK   ST. LOUIS   SAN FRANCISCO
TORONTO   LONDON   SYDNEY

STREAMS

their dynamics and morphology

Library of Congress Catalog Card Number
68-12267

07-043123-X
07-043124-8

11121314151617 MUMU 765

PREFACE

While pursuing my studies of rivers in the field, I found there were regions, even in these United States, where people believed that floods and stream erosion were acts of a supernatural hand and man could not (and should not) interfere or try to control them.

How true, then, is Loren Eiseley's statement that water must contain magic. For magic connotes secret forces, forces not understood, forces beyond ordinary human control. This book is an attempt to explain some of those "secret" forces by which water works, because it is only by understanding that man can eventually live in harmony with nature. Man's attempts to control rivers have often had little or no success. In fact, many times his efforts have aggravated the situation. The greatest natural disasters come as a result of ignorance or, even worse, half-knowledge. Hence a real understanding of the dynamic principles guiding the activity of rivers is necessary so that we may work along with these forces.

However, the magic of water goes beyond the physical processes of river hydraulics. The magic of life itself is in water. For it was in the water that life began, and, although later life moved from the sea to the land, living things never lost their dependence on water. So man himself depends upon water to sustain his life. But those springs and streams on which he relies are disappearing as a source of life because of his own thoughtless use and pollution. Thus, man's continued existence depends in great part on his understanding rivers—their morphology and dynamics.

So this book was written in an attempt to explain away some of the mystery of rivers, and to explain in terms which are understandable with little or no previous knowledge of the subject. The need is great, and I hope this book in some way fulfills it.

My sincere thanks go to some good friends and very severe critics, Irene Waraksa and Sonny Montgomery, for their critical reading of the manuscript. If the text is clear and simple it is because they made me explain and reexplain. And my thanks to Stanley Schumm for his valuable criticisms and suggestions. Much of the credit must be given to these three people for the good points of the text. Any blame for its failings are mine alone. My appreciation, also, to Mr. and Mrs. Grafly Dougherty for supplying some photographs and photographic work. To my family and many other friends who gave continuous encouragement in this undertaking, my thanks for their patience and support. And, finally, I would like to extend thanks for the inspiration provided by Prof. A. N. Strahler, who introduced me to the fascination of quantitative geomorphology.

Marie Morisawa

CONTENTS

LIST OF ILLUSTRATIONS

1

Introduction

The most important of all the geologic processes is running water. Rivers play an important part, not only in the shaping of the earth's surface, but also in the shaping of man's life on the earth. Ancient civilizations flourished on the banks of the Tigris and the Nile Rivers, large cities grew up along the great streams of countries throughout the world, and rivers provided the pathways by which man, in the past and even now, has penetrated the wilderness.

The 10 largest rivers of the world are listed in Table 1.1. They are presented in order of amount of discharge, i.e., the volume of water flowing through a cross section of the stream channel per unit time, measured in cubic feet per second (cfs). The Amazon River is by far the greatest in the world in amount of discharge and drainage area. Each of the rivers is of great importance for the nation or nations through which it flows.

2   *Streams*

Table 1.1   Ten Largest Rivers of the World

	Length, mi*	Area, 1,000 mi^2†	Discharge, 1,000 cfs†
Amazon	3,900	2,368	4,000–5,000‡
Congo	2,900	1,550	1,400
Yangtze	3,600	750	770
Mississippi-Missouri	3,890	1,244	620§
Yenisei	2,800	1,000	615
Lena	2,660	936	547
Paraná	1,500	890	526
Ob	3,200	959	441
Amur	2,900	712	338
Nile	4,160	1,150	100

* Data (rounded off) from the Encyclopaedia Britannica (1960), vol. 19, p. 326.
† Data from L. B. Leopold, Rivers: Am. Scientist, vol. 50, no. 4, 1962.
‡ Recent measurements indicate that the Amazon may carry as much as 11 percent of the average annual world runoff, which would give 4 to 5 million cfs. (R. E. Oltman, H. O'R. Sternberg, F. C. Ames, and L. C. Davis, Jr.: Amazon River investigations, reconnaissance measurements of July 1963, U.S. Geol. Surv. Circ. 486.)
§ From U.S. Geol. Surv. Circ. 44.

Wide valleys floored with fertile sediment, the energy and power of a swift-moving current, and the life-giving qualities of water itself, all these have made rivers the center of man's life and progress.

The source of streamflow

Although man has always so depended upon rivers, it has taken him a long time to understand them. Such a simple matter as the source of the water in streams was not solved quantitatively until the seventeenth century. The great Greek philosopher and natural scientist, Aristotle, clearly conceived the idea of the meteorological cycle of evaporation of water by heat and its cooling to form rain, and he applied this theory to the formation of water within the earth. He believed that the coolness in the earth condensed the water vapor in the pores of the soil and that this water, so formed, collected and flowed out as springs. He also realized that when it rained in high areas the water was absorbed by the ground and came to the surface lower down the slope as springs.

But although Aristotle evidently observed that some streams resulted from percolation of rain, he could not believe that there was enough rain to supply water for all the streams which flowed the year round. As Seneca, a first-century Roman, expressed it, rain "can only enlarge and quicken" the flow of a stream. And though a glimmering of the recognition of the true source of river water is shown in the writings of a contemporary of Seneca, Vitruvius, and by Leonardo da Vinci, natural scientists of the Middle Ages believed the source to be water beneath the earth, supplied from the oceans.

It was Bernard Palissy who, in the sixteenth century, stated that all springs are fed by rain and only rain.

When I had long and closely examined the source of the springs of natural fountains, and the place whence they could come, I finally understood that they could not come from or be produced by anything but rains . . . cliffs and mountains retain water as a bronze vessel would. And these waters, falling on these mountains, through the ground and cracks, always descend and do not stop until . . . having found some channel or other opening, they flow out as fountains or brooks or rivers.[1]

He arrived at these conclusions from observing that there are far more springs on mountain slopes than down in the valleys. If spring water came from the ocean lying beneath the surface of the land, it could never rise that high but would flow out lower down wherever there were cracks. Moreover, if springs came from the sea, why should they dry up in the summer? After all, the ocean is always there, with no noticeable change in level, winter

[1] The admirable discourses of Bernard Palissy, translated by A. LaRocque: University of Illinois Press, Urbana, Ill., 1957, pp. 48, 56.

or summer. And, finally, water derived from the sea should be salty and spring water was not.

But Palissy did not convince the natural scientists, and it was not until 1674 that proof was provided that there was enough rainfall to keep a stream flowing steadily. Pierre Perrault measured the precipitation in the Seine basin and compared it with the amount of runoff in the river. He found that six times as much rain fell on the watershed as flowed out in the stream channel. Not only was there enough rain to supply the stream: there was more than enough.

The origin of stream valleys

It took man much longer to recognize the erosive ability of streams, although Aristotle, Avicenna, and others did realize that streams carved the surface of the earth and made the landscape. In the Middle Ages, science was fostered by the Church and religious influences supported the hypothesis of a ready-made world whose surface was changeable only by catastrophic action. Many natural scientists thought that the Mosaic flood was the final and greatest event in a series of floods, earthquakes, and other disasters that had shaped the earth's features. Such persons were called *cataclysmists* or *catastrophists*. This idea was held by most of the natural scientists of the seventeenth and eighteenth centuries and even by many of the nineteenth.

However, there were some dissenters. Agricola described very clearly how running water cuts a channel, widens it, and then forms a floodplain.

The little brooks first wash away the surface soil and then cut into the solid rock and carrying it away grain by grain finally cut even a mountain range in two. . . . In a few years they thus dig a deep depression or river bed across a level or gently sloping plain. . . . In the course of years these stream beds reach an astonishing depth, while their banks rise up majestically on either side. . . . When the mountain cliffs on either side have become progressively lowered in height, wide valleys are formed and in them fertile fields appear bordering the stream.

At this stage the mountain lies back from the stream on either margin of the valley. . . . This is because the stream wears away its banks, sometimes only one of them which is made of softer materials and at other times both banks. The material which it removes from its banks it deposits either in its bed or carries it off downstream to lay it down somewhere else. . . . It will eat into the softer portions of the bank and be deflected away from the harder. And so we see that the stream will assume a sinuous course, and now swinging from side to side will incise a new bed for itself, and abandon its former one. This process results in making the valley wider still. In this way whole mountains are destroyed by the action of water and their debris scattered far and wide.[2]

The idea of stream sculpture was thoroughly developed by a number of natural scientists in the eighteenth century. Guettard's work in the Paris basin and his paper on the degradation of mountains dealt with the erosive ability of running water. Desmarest traced the history and development of a landscape in the Auverne of central France, showing that the valleys were formed by the streams which still occupied them. DeSaussure, working in the Alps, saw that the valleys and drainage systems of the region were very closely related to each other. But, despite the writings and observations of these men, the idea persisted that valleys were the result of catastrophic action. Streams flowed there only because the valley was already formed and ready.

At the close of the eighteenth century, Hutton and Playfair refuted the cataclysmic notion and clearly set forth the principle that streams do erode their own valleys. If a catastrophe formed a valley, it should be straight and should have no branching tributary valleys. The irregular pattern of a drainage system therefore shows that the valleys must have been cut by flowing water. Also, valleys generally become smaller as the valley bottoms rise in elevation, and this they correlated with the decrease in amount of stream-flow toward the head. This "erroneous and unscientific viewpoint" was immediately repudiated, for it was obvious that many rivers are depositing in, and filling up, the valleys in which they flow.

[2] From Frank Dawson Adams, The birth and development of the geological sciences: Dover, New York, 1938, p. 343.

Thus, in the first quarter of the nineteenth century, many geologists still ascribed the origin of stream gorges to a structural feature. Valleys were formed, not by erosion, but by faulting or folding. As late as 1815 the Niagara gorge was stated to have been formed by a dreadful catastrophe. Gradually, however, with the spread of Hutton's ideas and the gathering of more data and examples, the fact that rivers do erode the valleys in which they flow was generally accepted. Newberry, a geologist with an early expedition up the Colorado River, described the massive gorges of the Colorado Plateau region as canyons of river erosion.

Like the great cañons of the Colorado, the broad valleys bounded by high and perpendicular walls belong to a vast system of erosion and are wholly due to the action of water. . . . Examining with all possible care the structure of the great cañons which we entered, I everywhere found evidence of the exclusive action of water in their formation.[3]

The cycle of stream erosion

Newberry was only one of the many geologists exploring the western United States. Others were G. K. Gilbert and J. W. Powell, who in their descriptions and examples demonstrated some of the fundamental laws of river action and from whose writings many of our geologic terms and ideas are derived. Powell originated the concept of a base level of stream erosion, from which has grown the formulation of the cycle of erosion with ultimate peneplanation. He also described drainage systems, using the words *antecedent* and *consequent*. Gilbert showed great insight in his analysis of the erosive and transportive power of rivers. He was greatly concerned with these processes and studied them in detail, not only in natural streams, but also in laboratory flumes. Much of his work is still valid and will be described later in this book.

Taking the ideas of these men and others, W. M. Davis systematized and integrated them into a geomorphic principle of fluvial

[3] J. H. Newberry, Colorado River of the west: Am. J. Sci., vol. 33, p. 398, 1862.

denudation known as the *erosion cycle*. A stream goes through successive periods of development called *youth, maturity,* and *old age*. A stream is young if it has a torrential current flowing down an irregular slope, generally over falls and rapids, and enclosed in a steep-walled, V-shaped valley. It is characterized by a load that is small in amount but large in particle size. According to Davis, such a youthful stream has an excess of energy over the work it has to do, i.e., the load it has to carry; hence this excess energy is used to downcut the channel bed. As a result of downcutting, the gradient of the stream progressively decreases with time, thus diminishing the total amount of energy until it equals just the amount needed to transport the load. The stream has now reached maturity, a stage which is characterized by a gentle, smooth gradient and widened valley. It is during this stage that a stream fills its valley with deposits, upon which it begins to meander and erodes sideways, encroaching on the valley walls. Thus a stream approaches old age, a time of sluggish flow, with the river meandering on a wide, open floodplain, incapable of carrying anything except a small amount of fine debris. Since its exposition by Davis in 1899, the idea of a stream cycle has dominated thinking in fluvial geomorphology. It is only in recent times, with the advent of quantitative methods in stream studies, that this traditional concept is changing.

Development of river hydraulics

Streams have also been studied by hydraulic engineers, not because of interest in the processes of denudation and formation of the surface features of the earth, but because of the necessary part that rivers play in the life of man. Streams had to be controlled in times of flood, they had to be kept open for navigation, they had to be harnessed for energy, and they had to be stored for use. To these ends, rivers were intensively studied to find answers to the engineering problems which arose. Before the nineteenth century, Surell studied the rushing torrents of the French Alps, Daussé formulated some principles of equilibrium of rivers, and Sternberg published work relating the gradient of a stream to the abrasion of grains carried in its load. Both DuBoys and Guerard studied the Rhone, inquiring into the way in which the river transported its load of debris. Only a few of the many engineering studies can even be mentioned here. Toward the end of the nineteenth century, the Mississippi River Commission was established to study ways to improve the river for navigation and for flood-control purposes. Also, about this time scale models began to be used for stream research.

A massive amount of literature also appeared in the early twentieth century, mostly as a result of the need for irrigation and storage. British engineers in India, Egypt, and other parts of the arid and semiarid regions concentrated on the design and problems of irrigation canals. Kennedy, Buckley, Bligh, and Lindley are just a few of those who worked on the development of channels that would not be silted up or eroded. In so doing, they drew up empirical relationships of velocity, width, depth, and other stream characteristics to stream discharge. Such studies, though adding to our fund of basic knowledge, resulted mainly in solutions to specific problems which were applicable only to the streams, canals, and circumstances concerned. However, these results, together with data from other river and model studies, do supply facts from which general theories can be developed.

Development of fluid mechanics

Parallel with advances in empirical hydraulics and in the descriptive geomorphology of streams, mathematicians and physicists were developing rational theories of fluid mechanics to explain the flow of stream water. Bernoulli discussed the energy of flow even before the basic principles of hydromechanics were stated by the founder of the science, Euler, in 1755. DeChézy proposed a formula for streamflow in 1775 which is still used today. The nineteenth century brought many advances, among them Boussinesq's theory of flowing water in terms of viscous stresses and Reynolds' idea of turbulent motion. Great strides have been made in the twentieth century in this science as a result of the impetus to the study of the fluid motion of air given by the invention of the airplane.

Quantitative geomorphology

Thus the basis for a quantitative study of streams and their description was established by hydraulic engineers and physicists. But these men are not generally interested in cause and effect: they are concerned with an immediate problem and are seeking an empirical and often expedient solution. It is the geomorphologists who seek cause and effect, who try to explain the processes by which running water creates landforms. In the past, geomorphology was mainly concerned with streams from a descriptive point of view: they were young, mature, or old; they had V-shaped valleys. However, some geomorphologists, dissatisfied with this approach, are now trying to define and describe rivers and fluvial morphology in more rigorous and mathematical terms. They feel that a quantitative approach will throw more light on the processes and mechanics operating in natural streams, since measurement will show the magnitude of variables involved. To understand fully and interpret landforms, a knowledge of the physical principles by which a river operates is necessary. The purpose of this book is to bring before the beginning student some basic principles of fluid mechanics, open-channel hydraulics, and hydrology in simple, compact form and to introduce him to some of the quantitative work that has been done recently in geomorphology.

REFERENCES AND SELECTED READINGS

Adams, F. D. (1938) The birth and development of the geological sciences: Dover, New York.

Davis, W. M. (1909) Geographical essays: Ginn, Boston (republished 1954, Dover, New York).

LaRocque, A. (1957) The admirable discourses of Bernard Palissy: University of Illinois Press, Urbana, Ill.

Newberry, J. H. (1862) Colorado River of the west: Am. J. Sci., vol. 33, p. 398.

Playfair, J. (1802) Illustrations of the Huttonian theory of the earth: Cadell and Davies, London.

Powell, J. W. (1876) Report on the geology of the eastern portion of the Uinta Mts., Geographical and geological survey of the Rocky Mt. Region: GPO, Washington.

Rouse, H. (1938) Fluid mechanics for hydraulic engineers: McGraw-Hill, New York.

2

Hydrology

According to the dictionary, a stream is a flow of running water, large or small, and a river is a large stream of water. Most geologists use the terms interchangeably to denote running water of any size, but the word *river* is often reserved to denote the main stream or larger branches of a drainage system. Geomorphologically, the words apply exclusively to channelized flow and, indeed, may refer to channels without water. Such streams, consisting of a dry channel throughout most of the year, bearing water only during and immediately after a rain, are called *ephemeral.* Stream channels which carry water part of the year and are dry the other part, but which receive flow from the groundwater table when it is high enough, are called *intermittent.* Those streams which carry water the year round, being fed by a fairly stable groundwater flow, are called *perennial.*

The hydrologic cycle

It was Bernard Palissy who reasonably explained that springs have their origin in and are fed by rain and rain alone. He also showed how this happens: sea water evaporates, is condensed to form rain, which falls, percolates into the ground, and emerges later as springs and rivers, which return the water to the sea. This is the so-called *hydrologic cycle*, a term still used today to express the balance in the different forms of water in the air, on land, and in the sea.

Water evaporates from all surface waters and from the soil, is condensed, and falls as some sort of precipitation, rain, snow, sleet, or hail. The precipitation is distributed in several ways: some flows off immediately as surface runoff into brooks, streams, and rivers; some infiltrates through the ground and joins a river or emerges as a spring; some of this may be stored in the ground as groundwater, and some may remain in the soil as soil moisture. Part of the precipitation may be returned to the air immediately by evaporation, and part may be retained on the surface in lakes or ponds (detention storage), to be evaporated later. Still another part may be caught by plants and transpired or stored in the roots or may enter the plant tissue, not to be returned to the cycle until the death of the vegetation.

The hydrologic cycle is sometimes expressed mathematically as

$$RF = RO + ET \qquad (2.1)$$

where RF includes all types of precipitation, RO is runoff, and ET is evapotranspiration. Runoff refers to the total amount of water which reaches the stream, including immediate surface runoff, plus the rainfall which joins the stream later by infiltration.

Runoff-rainfall relationships

Total runoff, or streamflow, then, depends on the factors of rainfall and evapotranspiration. Over the world, which has approximately 40 in. of rainfall, it is generally estimated that about 20 percent of this becomes runoff. These averages for world runoff are highly theoretical for the data are scant and generalized. Runoff in the United States can be determined much more accurately because of the great number of streams whose flow is measured by the Geological Survey. Over the United States as a whole, about one-third of the rainfall becomes runoff, although this figure varies greatly in different parts of the country. Table 2.1 shows the areal distribution of runoff in the United States. The figures indicate that slightly over half the area of the country has an annual runoff of less than 5 in., with an overall average runoff annually of 8.7 in. During this same period of time the mean yearly rainfall was about 30 in.

Table 2.1 Areal Distribution of Run-off in the United States, 1921–1945

Range in runoff, in.	% total area
0.0 – 0.25	10.1
0.25– 0.5	12.6
0.5 – 1.0	8.8
1.0 – 2.5	13.7
2.5 – 5.0	8.2
5.0 –10.0	8.5
10.0 –20.0	27.5
20.0 –40.0	9.6
40.0 –80.0	1.0

Source: From W. B. Langbein and others, Annual runoff in the United States: U.S. Geol. Surv. Circ. 52, 1949.

The 10 largest rivers of the United States ranked by amount of discharge are shown in Table 2.2. Drainage area and longest stream length from head to mouth are also shown. Of these 10 rivers, 7 are part of the Mississippi River watershed, a system which accounts for over one-third the total runoff of the United States. Some rivers may drain larger areas than those in this table,

Table 2.2   Ten Largest Rivers of the United States (in Discharge)

River	Mean Annual Discharge, cfs	Drainage area, mi^2	River length, mi
Mississippi*	620,000	1,243,700	3,892
Ohio*	255,000	203,900	1,306
Columbia	235,000	258,200	1,214
Yukon	150,000	330,000	2,300+
Mississippi* (above the Missouri)	91,300	171,600	1,170
Missouri*	70,000	529,400	2,714
Tennessee*	63,700	40,600	900
Mobile	59,000	42,300	758
Red*	57,300	91,400	1,300
Arkansas*	42,200	160,500	1,450

* Part of the greater Mississippi drainage system.
Source: From Large rivers of the United States: U.S. Geol. Surv. Circ. 44, prepared by the Water Resources Division, 1949.

but they have lower discharges. For example, the Rio Grande River basin would be seventh in basin size among the rivers of Table 2.2, but it is not shown there because it has an annual discharge less than 10,000 cfs. Other rivers which drain a larger area than either the Mobile or Tennessee Rivers in the table, but which have a small mean annual discharge, are shown in Table 2.3. These streams all flow through regions which have a low average yearly rainfall. The Colorado River, which is not included in any of these tables, has an area of 137,000 square miles and an annual mean discharge of only 17,000 cfs.

The relationship between rainfall and runoff in a specific drainage basin is illustrated by the graph in Fig. 2.1. The fact that there seems to be a straight-line relationship between these two factors in almost all basins studied has resulted in the attempt to predict the runoff with a given amount of rain. This can be done by drawing the regression line which best fits all the points on the graph and then from a specific rainfall reading off the expected runoff. For example, in Fig. 2.1, one would predict about 2.0 in. of runoff in the Neosho River basin if there were a rainfall of 28 in. This is an empirical relationship, and the particular regres-

Table 2.3 Large Rivers of the United States with Mean Annual Discharge Less Than 10,000 cfs

River	Area, mi^2
Rio Grande	171,585
Platte	90,000
Kansas	61,300
Gila	58,100
Brazos	44,500

Source: From Large rivers of the United States: U.S. Geol. Surv. Circ. 44, prepared by the Water Resources Division, 1949.

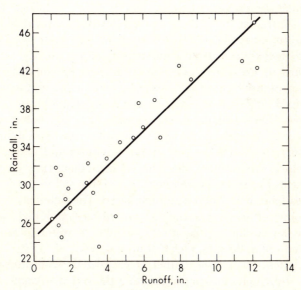

Fig. 2.1 The relationship between rainfall and runoff in the Neosho River above Iola, Kans. Note the wide scatter of points, which indicates that factors other than rainfall probably influence runoff. [Redrawn from Hoyt and others (1936).]

sion line applies only to the particular watershed. Similar graphs and regressions of rainfall and runoff can be drawn up for other drainage basins.

Evapotranspiration

The uniqueness of the runoff-rainfall relationship for each basin is a result of the fact that streamflow is influenced by factors other than rainfall alone. It is really determined by the amount of rainfall excess, i.e., rainfall which does not sink into the ground and is not stored on the surface. Rainfall excess is determined primarily by climate, vegetation, infiltration capacity, and surface storage. Important climatic elements are amount, duration, intensity, and time distribution of rain in a particular basin. Insolation, temperature, humidity, and wind affect total evaporation, soil moisture, and vegetative growth—and thus affect runoff. Vegetation influences runoff by providing interception of water by foliage, by promoting infiltration in slowing up and dividing surface flow, and by contributing to detention storage in holding water on the surface. Its effect varies with type and density of growth.

The loss of water by transpiration and its use in plant tissue, and evaporation from water surfaces, soil pores, and snow, are all grouped together as total evaporation, evapotranspiration, or water loss. These factors are very hard to measure, but some data have been gathered by using evaporating pans and lysimeters. Lysimeters are containers with watertight sides and pervious bottoms, which are set into the ground with their rims flush with the surface. The water percolating through the soil in the container can be caught at the bottom and measured. The difference between the amount of water entering at the surface and that draining through the bottom represents the amount of water taken up by plants and soil in the plot, plus that evaporated.

Most often, evapotranspiration is calculated by measuring the amount of precipitation and subtracting the gaged streamflow. Figure 2.2 illustrates the relationship of rainfall, runoff, and water loss in selected watersheds. In this figure, water loss (evapotranspiration) is found by subtracting runoff from rainfall. The Dela-

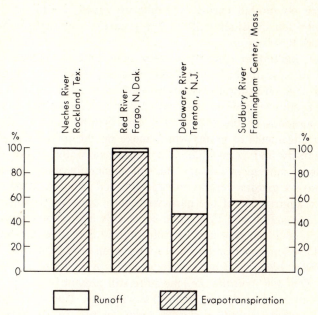

Fig. 2.2 The proportion of rainfall lost by evapotranspiration and that part which is runoff, for selected river basins. Evapotranspiration calculated by subtracting measured runoff from measured rainfall. [Data from Williams and others (1940).]

ware River basin is one of the few where runoff is more than 50 percent of the rainfall. The Red River represents the other extreme, where runoff is a minor part of the cycle and most of the rain that falls is lost by evaporation and transpiration.

Infiltration capacity

Infiltration capacity is the rate at which water will be absorbed by a soil. It starts with an initial value, decreases rapidly, then reaches a steady value which is the infiltration capacity of the given soil. Rainfall occurring after a steady rate of infiltration is reached is rainfall excess and flows off as surface runoff. A rain which falls with an intensity less than infiltration capacity will produce no rainfall excess and thus no runoff, because the rate of infiltration of water will be less than the capacity of the soil to absorb it.

Thus, infiltration capacity is very important in controlling the runoff of a watershed. The infiltration capacity of a given soil during a given rainstorm is determined by soil texture, soil structure, vegetative cover, biologic structures, antecedent soil moisture, and conditions of the soil surface. *Soil texture* refers to the size and arrangements of grains which make up the soil. It determines the porosity and permeability, or volume of water absorbed and its rate of movement through the soil. Generally, more permeable soils have a greater infiltration capacity. *Soil structure* denotes the state of aggregation of soil particles. Loose, open aggregations promote high infiltration. *Vegetative cover* aids infiltration by preserving loose soil structure and by diffusing the flow of water, increasing infiltration opportunity. Plant roots, worm borings, animal holes, and other *biologic structures* help increase infiltration capacity. *Antecedent soil moisture,* i.e., moisture still present from a previous rain, will tend to lower infiltration capacity. However, extreme dryness, where the *soil surface* is baked or compacted, lowers the ability of the soil to absorb water. Rain itself can reduce infiltration capacity by packing the soil, breaking down the structure of aggregates, washing down finer grains to fill the pores, and swelling colloids and clay by wetting them.

Storm rainfall and runoff

The disposition of storm rainfall is shown in Fig. 2.3. From this it can be seen that streamflow is composed of several elements: rain falling in the channel, excess rainfall or surface runoff, interflow, and groundwater. The figure is diagrammatic and gives only a very generalized picture. The actual amounts of rainfall distributed in the ways shown vary with each basin. Rain falling directly into the channel does not usually represent a very large part of the total rainfall. Surface runoff, which occurs only when rainfall exceeds the infiltration rate, is the first major element of streamflow to reach a river. It is the main component of flood and peak dis-

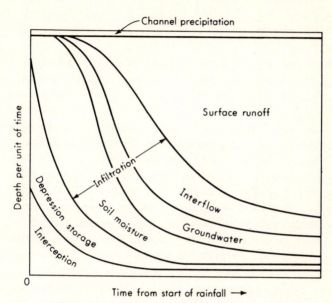

Fig. 2.3 Disposition of storm rainfall into its component parts.
This is diagrammatic and not to scale. [Redrawn from Linsley,
Kohler, and Paulhus (1949).]

charges during a rainstorm. The next element which contributes
to the volume of flow is interflow, i.e., water which infiltrates the
soil and moves laterally toward the stream channel. The amount
of interflow, with movement entirely above the groundwater table,
is increased by the presence of an impervious layer which will
limit percolation to the groundwater table and force the water
to move laterally. The total amount which interflow contributes
to streamflow depends upon the soil structure and the depth to
the groundwater table. The stable element of streamflow is groundwater, which is the result of gravity percolation downward to the
groundwater table, a region of saturation. Because of the influx
of water during a storm, not only does the top level of the water
table rise, but there is also a movement of groundwater toward
the stream. This discharge of groundwater from the zone of saturation into the channel takes place over a long period of time
and supplies the steady year-round flow of streams. It is not an
important contributor to flood peaks.

Effect of geology

Each of the aforementioned factors is greatly influenced by the topographic (physiographic) and geologic conditions of the watershed. Altitude and orientation of the basin, shape and ground slope of the watershed, relief, rock type and soil mantle, and geologic structure are all important elements in determining the hydrologic characteristics of a river system. The effects of altitude and orientation are mainly climatic. There are an increase in precipitation and a decrease in temperature with increased altitude which generally result in higher runoff. This applies only as high as the snow line, however, since above that the loss of moisture by sublimation of snow tends to diminish total runoff. Orientation of a watershed may influence the amount both of precipitation and of insolation. For example, in an area where the movement of air masses is from west to east, a north-south-trending mountain range will have a rainy west side and a dry eastern slope. Observation has shown that watersheds on north-facing slopes, in general, have a larger amount of runoff and better-developed drainage systems than those on southerly slopes. This is primarily because of the difference in insolation and, hence, evaporation.

The shape of a basin is important because it influences the time distribution of runoff. In a long, narrow basin, flow in tributary channels reaches the main stream at different times, thus distributing the total runoff over a long span of time. In a wide, square, or fan-shaped basin, tributaries feed into the main-trunk stream at the same time and tend to produce a sudden high peak flow.

Generally, direct runoff decreases with decreased steepness of the ground surface. A gentle slope should allow more opportunity for infiltration and detention storage than a steep one. Also, flatter areas are more densely vegetated, in general, than extremely steep ones, and vegetation diminishes runoff.

The rock type and soil mantle affect infiltration capacity. A permeable soil or rock allows the water to percolate to the groundwater table, where it is slowly discharged into streams. Thus direct surface runoff is lowered, but not the final total amount. Basins on bedrock or soil which is nonabsorptive have a high volume of direct runoff and very little groundwater flow. The attitude or structure of the bedrock is important in that it not only affects the topography but also directly affects the disposal of storm rainfall by determining the drainage pattern and basin shape.

Measurement of streamflow

One of the chief concerns of hydrologists is the measurement of, and relationships among, the various forms of water in the hydrologic cycle. Streamflow can be measured more exactly than evaporation, transpiration, or rainfall. Hence the collection and interpretation of streamflow data are very important. The U.S. Geological Survey maintains over 6,000 stations in the United States where streamflow is gaged. The flow is measured by recording the stage, or height in feet of the surface of the water above an arbitrary datum. By using an equation

$$Q = AV \tag{2.2}$$

where Q is discharge in cubic feet per second, A is cross-sectional area of the channel where measurements are being taken, and V is mean velocity at the measured cross section, discharge can be calculated for different measured cross sections and velocities at different water levels. Then a graphic relationship is drawn up between stage and discharge as in Fig. 2.4. From this rating curve it is possible to read the discharge for any measured gage height.

Stream hydrographs

The hydrograph of a river is a graph which shows how the streamflow varies with time. As such, it reflects those characteristics of the watershed which influence runoff. A hydrograph may show yearly, monthly, daily, or instantaneous discharges. From them one can determine the total flow, base (groundwater) flow, and periods of high and low flows. Long-period hydrographs are used in the design of irrigation and power developments and in water-supply and flood forecasting. Figure 2.5 shows a hydrograph of mean monthly discharges for a portion of the Allegheny River basin over the period of a water year.

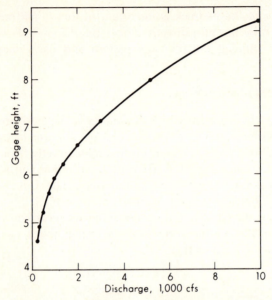

Fig. 2.4 Stage-discharge rating curve for the Allegheny River near Kinzua, Pa., showing the relationship between height of water at gage and amount of discharge. (Data from Water Supply Paper 1143.)

A hydrograph for the same basin during a particular storm is shown in Fig. 2.6. The storm was a violent one and brought on one of the highest floods in the Allegheny River at Eldred, Pa. This hydrograph may be described as a flashy one with a sharp, high peak. Since the shape of the storm hydrograph depends upon the features of a watershed which determine the disposition of storm rainfall, its interpretation is an important tool in the analysis of stream and basin characteristics. The rising limb of the curve is generally concave upward and reflects the infiltration capacity of a watershed. The time before the steep climb represents the time before infiltration capacity is reached. A sudden, steeply rising limb reflects great immediate surface runoff and very little absorption, whatever the reason. The crest, or peak, of the curve marks the maximum runoff. Some basins may have two or more peaks for a single storm, depending upon the time distribution of the rain and basin characteristics. With the same storm, a watershed

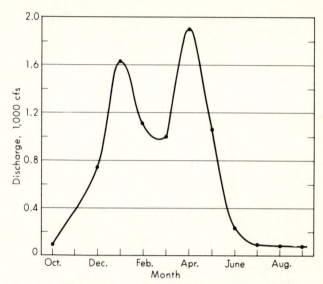

Fig. 2.5 Hydrograph of the Allegheny River at Eldred, Pa., for the water year 1948–1949. Peak flows occurred during January and April–May. River discharge is dependent upon base (groundwater) flow from mid-June to October. (Data from Water Supply Paper 1143.)

with large storage capacity and absorptive surface or channel has a lower peak than a watershed with little storage capacity. The recession curve represents the outflow from basin storage after inflow has ceased. Its slope is therefore dependent upon the physical characteristics which determine storage.

Analytical methods have been developed by hydrologists to separate the storm hydrograph into its component parts so that the specific contributions of surface runoff, interflow, and groundwater flow to the total runoff can be determined. These storm hydrographs can also be used to predict the passage of flood waves.

Flow-duration curves

Another type of graph which can be drawn from streamflow data is a cumulative frequency, or flow-duration, curve which shows

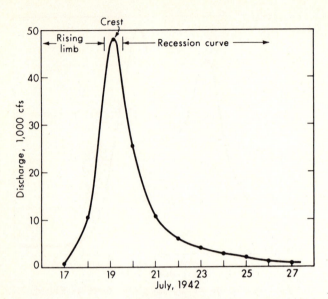

Fig. 2.6 Hydrograph of the Allegheny River at Eldred, Pa., during a storm of July 17–19, 1942. [Data from Eisenlohr (1952).]

the percent of time a specified discharge is equaled or exceeded. To prepare such a curve, all flows during a given period are listed according to their magnitude and tallied. The percent of time each was equaled or exceeded is then calculated and plotted. A flow-duration curve from Bowie Creek, Miss., is shown in Fig. 2.7. From this we can see that 50 percent of the time the creek has a discharge of 250 cfs or more.

The shape of the flow-duration curve gives some clue as to the characteristics of the drainage basin. If the curve has an overall steep slope, the watershed is one with a large amount of direct runoff. If the curve is fairly flat, there is substantial storage, either on the surface or as groundwater, which tends to equalize the flow. This type of flow curve has been used to determine the possibility of waterpower and in stream-pollution studies. It can also be used as a basis for comparison of different rivers to show the effects of geology.

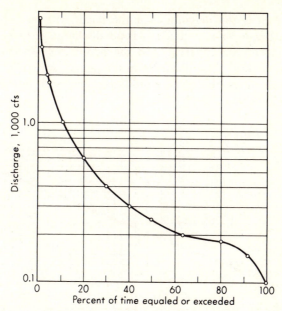

Fig. 2.7 Duration curve, daily flow, for Bowie Creek near Hattiesburg, Miss., for the period 1939–1948. [Redrawn from Searcy (1959).]

Flood-frequency analysis

Perhaps the greatest immediate practical use of stream-gaging data and hydrograph analysis is to provide a knowledge of the magnitude and probable frequency of floods. To draw up a flood-frequency analysis, one can use either the maximum discharge for each year or all discharges greater than a given discharge, irrespective of year. These peak discharges are listed according to magnitude, with the highest discharge first. Next the recurrence interval, i.e., the period of years within which a flood of given magnitude or greater will occur, is determined by the equation

$$T = \frac{n+1}{m} \tag{2.3}$$

where T is the recurrence interval, n is the number of years of record, and *m* is the magnitude of the flood, with *m* = 1 at the highest discharge on record. Each flood discharge is then plotted against its recurrence interval, and the points are joined to form the frequency curve (Fig. 2.8). From this graph, we could predict that every 8 years the river would have a flood discharge of 20,000 cfs or more.

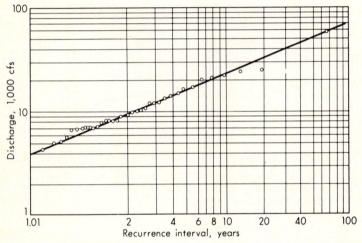

Fig. 2.8 Flood-frequency curve of the Licking River, Tobaso, Ohio. [After Dalrymple (1960).]

To understand rivers fully, then, we must first learn about the water in them. And much of the understanding we seek comes from the analysis of records of climate and weather, of streamflow gaging, and of groundwater measurements. All these data when collected, collated, and interpreted correctly will help us toward our goal, for the various forms of water in the hydrologic cycle may end up as streamflow. Only that part of precipitation that is evaporated or transpired back into the air is lost to the river. The rest of the rain or snow may pause along the way in ponds, in the soil, or as groundwater, but it will eventually seek the ocean via a river channel.

REFERENCES AND SELECTED READINGS

Corbett, D. M. (1943) Stream gaging procedure: U.S. Geol. Surv. Water Supply Paper 888.

Dalrymple, T. (1960) Flood frequency analyses: U.S. Geol. Surv. Water Supply Paper 1543A.

Eisenlohr, W. S., Jr. (1952) Floods of July 1942 in north-central Pennsylvania: U.S. Geol. Surv. Water Supply Paper 1134B.

Hoyt, W. G., and others (1936) Studies of relations of rainfall and runoff in the United States: U.S. Geol. Surv. Water Supply Paper 772.

Langbein, W. B., and others (1949) Annual runoff in the United States: U.S. Geol. Surv. Circ. 52.

Linsley, R. K., Jr., M. A. Kohler, and J. L. H. Paulhus (1949) Applied hydrology: McGraw-Hill, New York.

Searcy, J. M. (1959) Flow duration curves: U.S. Geol. Surv. Water Supply Paper 1542A.

Water Resources Division (1949) Large rivers of the United States: U.S. Geol. Surv. Circ. 44.

Water Resources Division (1952) Surface water supply of the United States, 1949. Part 3. The Ohio River basin: U.S. Geol. Surv. Water Supply Paper 1143.

Williams, G. R., and others (1940) Natural water loss in selected drainage basins: U.S. Geol. Surv. Water Supply Paper 846.

3

The hydraulics
of streams

Watching a stream, one sees a flow as change-able as the weather. Sometimes the water is smooth and clear, lazily swirling around an obstacle in its channel. At another time, it flows swiftly and darkly, carrying its murky load to the sea and sweeping everything before it. Still again, it may splash and tumble on its way, dancing and leaping over all obstructions. Thus a stream's flow varies, at one point as well as all along its path. However, for engineering purposes it is generally considered that, except at flood times, a stream has a steady, uniform flow. A steady flow is one in which, at any given point on a stream, the depth does not vary with time. And if the flow is uniform, the depth is constant over the length of the stream. Although these two assumptions are not strictly true, they allow simple and satisfactory solutions for river-engineering problems.

If, then, we assume a steady, uniform flow,

the rate at which water passes through successive cross sections of a stream (Fig. 3.1) is constant, or

$$A_1 V_1 = A_2 V_2 = Q \tag{3.1}$$

where A is the area of cross section at points 1 and 2, V is the mean velocity at those points, and Q is the constant discharge.

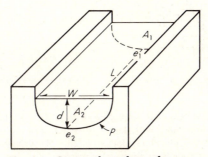

Fig. 3.1   Stream-channel morphometry. Stream width W is actual width of water in the channel. Wetted perimeter P is the outline of the edge where water and channel meet. Cross section A is the area of a transverse section of the river. Depth d is approximately the same as the hydraulic radius R, which is the cross section divided by the wetted perimeter ($R = A/P$). Stream gradient S is the drop in elevation ($e_1 - e_2$) between two points on the bottom of a channel, divided by the projected horizontal distance between them L. Velocity is the discharge per unit area.

Laminar flow

Water is a fluid, and, as such, it has the characteristic that it cannot resist stress. That is, any stress upon it, however small, causes

movement, with the water masses moving in laminar or turbulent
flow. If the water should flow along a smooth, straight channel
at very low velocities (fractions of a millimeter per second), it
would move in laminar flow, with parallel layers of water shearing
one over the other (Fig. 3.2a). Shearing stress is proportional to

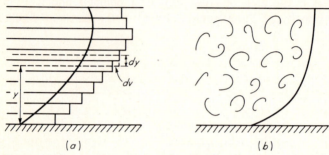

Fig. 3.2   Theoretical vertical profile of velocity. (*a*) is the velocity
profile of laminar flow, with layers of water shearing, one over the
other. (*b*) represents the velocity profile of turbulent flow with
chaotic movement of individual water masses.

the resistance of the fluid layers to movement. In this case, the
resistance is determined by viscosity (the stickiness caused by molecular friction between layers) and by the change in velocity from
one layer to the next. Thus, for Fig. 3.2a, at any point at a distance
y above the bed, where the layer of water is flowing at velocity
v, the shearing stress can be expressed as

$$\tau = \mu \frac{dv}{dy} \tag{3.2}$$

where τ is shearing stress, μ is viscosity, and dv/dy is the change
in velocity from one layer to the next (velocity gradient). In
laminar flow the layer of maximum velocity lies below the water
surface. At the boundary with bed or channel walls, velocity is
zero and increases with distance away from the boundary. Theoretically the paths of fluid movements are parallel and individual,

and there is no mixing. This type of flow cannot support solid particles in suspension and is not found in natural streams except near the bed and banks in the boundary layer, but it is common in groundwater flow.

Turbulent flow

When velocity exceeds a critical value, fluid flow becomes turbulent. This type of flow is characterized by a variety of chaotic movements, with secondary, heterogeneous eddies superimposed on the main forward flow. Any one fluid component follows a complex pattern of movement, and components mix with each other (Fig. 3.2b).

The factors which affect the critical velocity where laminar flow becomes turbulent are viscosity and density of the fluid, depth of water, and roughness of the channel surface. The more viscous the fluid, the higher the critical velocity at which flow becomes turbulent, since the stickiness will tend to keep the flow laminar. Water temperature also affects the critical velocity, for warmer fluids tend to be less viscous. The expression most commonly used to distinguish between laminar and turbulent flow is the Reynolds number,

$$N_R = \rho \, \frac{VR}{\mu} \qquad\qquad (3.3)$$

where ρ is density, V is mean velocity, R is hydraulic radius, and μ is viscosity. Flow is laminar for small values of the Reynolds number and turbulent for higher ones. The Reynolds number for flow in streams is generally over 500, varying from 300 to 600 with velocities of fractions of 1 mm/sec.

There are two kinds of turbulent flow, streaming and shooting flow. Streaming flow is the ordinary turbulence found in most streams, whereas shooting flow occurs at higher velocities, such as is found in rapids, and results in a great increase in the rate of erosion. Whether turbulent flow is shooting or streaming is determined by the Froude number F,

$$F = \frac{V}{\sqrt{gD}} \tag{3.4}$$

where V is mean velocity, g is the force of gravity, and D is the depth of water. If the Froude number is less than 1, the stream is in the tranquil- or streaming-flow regime. If F is greater than 1, the stream is in the rapid- or shooting-flow regime. Depth and velocity are the streamflow characteristics which determine the state of turbulent regime. When the flow of a stream changes from the streaming to the shooting state, the velocity increases greatly, and so there is a lowering of the water surface. When velocity is decelerated in the change from shooting to streaming flow, the water surface rises, causing stationary waves and backwater effects. The shearing force in turbulent flow can be expressed as

$$\tau = (\mu + \epsilon)\frac{dv}{dy} \tag{3.5}$$

where the symbols are as in Eq. (3.2) and ϵ is the eddy viscosity or exchange coefficient. Here we must take into account, not only the molecular friction μ as for laminar flow, but also the mixing and interaction of the fluid components. The exchange, or Austausch, coefficient ϵ is a measure of the intensity of turbulent mixing. The velocity profile of turbulent flow is somewhat smoothed by the mixing which occurs when fluid masses of one velocity are carried into regions of another velocity (Fig. 3.2b). The eddies move with the current and are modified and changed as they move by exchanging momentum, heat, dissolved-salt content, and suspended-sediment content with each other. The intensity of turbulence increases with increasing value of the Reynolds number; so the higher this is, the more uniform the velocity profile. The velocity of the water in contact with the bed is theoretically zero. Near the bed is a thin boundary layer of laminar flow which results from retardation of velocity by bed friction. The zone of maximum turbulence and mixing is above but near this bottom layer.

The thickness of the bottom laminar sublayer and its relationship to the size of particles on the bed determine the roughness of the flow. If the grain height is smaller than the thickness of the laminar layer, the smooth flow will extend higher up into the water. However, if many grains are large enough to project through the laminar sublayer, the flow is rough.

If the velocity distributions of various transverse cross sections are shown (Fig. 3.3), it will be seen that the lines of equal velocity

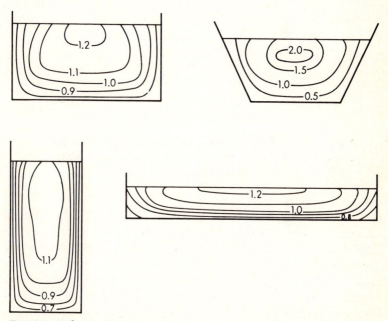

Fig. 3.3 Velocity distributions in transverse cross sections in channels of different shapes. Lines are isovels, i.e., lines of equal velocity. [After Lane (1937).]

(isovels) are closer together near the boundaries; in general, the highest isovel is in the center and is below or extends below the surface. Although the location of maximum velocity depends upon channel shape, roughness, and sinuosity, it usually lies at between 0.05 and 0.25 of the depth. Figure 3.4 shows the velocity profile

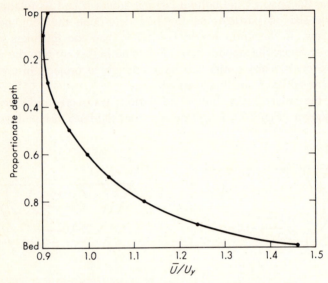

Fig. 3.4 Vertical velocity profile of the Mississippi River near Vicksburg, Miss. $\bar{U}/U_y$ is the ratio of average velocity to velocity at depth y. [Redrawn from Toffaleti (1963).]

of the Mississippi River near Vicksburg, Miss., with the point of maximum velocity at 0.1 of the depth below the surface. In the tabulation of these velocity measurements for the Mississippi, Toffaleti found that point velocities were more variable in the upper and lower depths, but were fairly stable in the middle region. Figure 3.5 illustrates how the velocity profile changes in moving from one bank across to the other. From this it can be seen that, in moving toward the center of a stream away from the banks, the point of maximum velocity rises toward the surface. Also, with a constant depth of flow, velocity increases toward the center of a river.

Leighley discussed the distribution of turbulence and velocity in stream channels from the ideal point of view. In a symmetrical river channel the maximum water velocity is below the surface and centered. Outward from the center of flow are regions of moderate velocity but high turbulence, greatest near the bottom. The

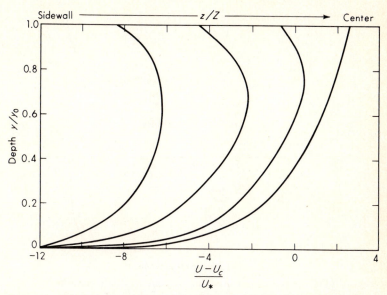

Fig. 3.5 Velocity distribution across a smooth, rectangular channel from bank to bank. z is distance from sidewall to the point; Z is distance from sidewall to center region boundary; y is depth to the point; y_0 is total depth; U is average velocity in a downstream direction; U_c is average velocity in central region of flow; and U_* is average shear velocity. [After Tracy and Lester (1961).]

parts of the stream flow near the channel walls have low velocities and low turbulence. However, in an asymmetrical channel, the zone of maximum velocity shifts away from the center toward the deeper side (Fig. 3.6). The zone of maximum turbulence is raised on the shallow side and lowered on the deeper side. Thus, significant erosive effects are brought about by change in channel morphology.

Stream energy

Turbulence and velocity are very closely related to the erosion, transportation, and deposition—or work—that a stream does. Work is measured by energy; so let us examine the energy of a river. There are two kinds of energy, potential and kinetic. Potential

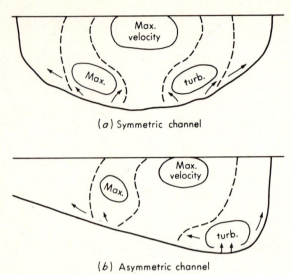

(*a*) Symmetric channel

(*b*) Asymmetric channel

Fig. 3.6. Zones of maximum velocity and turbulence in (*a*) symmetrical and (*b*) asymmetrical stream channels. [After Leighley (1934).]

energy is converted by downflow to kinetic energy, which, in turn, is mostly dissipated in heat of friction. Stream energy, then, is lost owing to friction from turbulent mixing. Hence, frictional heat losses depend upon channel characteristics of roughness, straightness, and cross-sectional form, as well as the amount of internal shearing of eddies. Energy which is not dissipated in heat is available for work, i.e., for erosion and transportation. However, it is thought that most of a stream's energy is lost, more than 95 percent being consumed in heat. The energy available for work can be increased if friction is decreased by smoothing or straightening the channel or by reducing the wetted perimeter. A minor loss of energy should result from inner friction of the load in transport, but generally a suspended load actually decreases friction because it decreases turbulence.

Potential energy is equal to the weight of water times the head, or difference in elevation of two points between which the energy is being calculated. Kinetic energy is equal to one-half the mass of water, times the square of the velocity at which the water is moving. In equation form

$$E_p = Wz \tag{3.6}$$

$$E_k = \frac{MV^2}{2} \tag{3.7}$$

where E_p is potential energy, E_k is kinetic energy, W is weight, z is head, M is mass, and V is velocity. Total energy, then, is influenced mostly by the velocity. Velocity, in turn, is a function of the gradient of a stream, the volume of water flowing, viscosity of water, and characteristics of the channel cross section and bed. This relationship has been expressed in several equations by hydraulic engineers.

One such equation is the Chézy formula, which expresses velocity as a function of hydraulic radius and slope,

$$V = C\sqrt{RS} \tag{3.8}$$

where V is mean velocity, R is hydraulic radius, S is slope, and C is a constant which depends upon gravity and other factors contributing to the friction force. Friction forces depend, you remember, upon roughness and straightness of the channel and its cross-sectional form.

The Manning formula is an attempt to refine the Chézy equation in terms of the constant C,

$$V = \frac{1.49}{n} R^{\frac{2}{3}} S^{\frac{1}{2}} \tag{3.9}$$

where the terms are the same as the Chézy equation and n is a roughness factor. The roughness factor has to be determined empirically and varies not only for different streams but also for the same stream under different conditions and at different times. The roughness coefficients of some natural streams are given in Table 3.1. Anything which affects the roughness of the channel changes n, including the size and shape of grains on the bed, sinuosity, obstructions in the channel such as vegetation, logs, piers, and sandbars, and any irregularity in channel section. Variation

Table 3.1 Values of Roughness Coefficient n *for Natural Streams*

Description of stream	normal n
On a plain:	
Clean straight channel, full stage, no riffs or deep pools	0.030
Same as above but with more stones and weeds	0.035
Clean winding channel, some pools and shoals	0.040
Sluggish reaches, weedy, deep pools	0.070
Mountain streams:	
No vegetation, steep banks, bottom of gravel, cobbles, and a few boulders	0.040
No vegetation, steep banks, bottom of cobbles, and large boulders	0.050
Floodplains:	
Pasture, no brush, short grass	0.030
Pasture, no brush, high grass	0.035
Brush, scattered to dense	0.050–0.10
Trees, dense to cleared, with stumps	0.150–0.04

Source: Data adapted from Chow (1959), pp. 112–113.

in discharge also affects *n*, since depth of water and volume influence the roughness.

Roughness due to obstacles on the bed or projections from the sidewalls causes a separation of flow and the formation of eddies (Fig. 3.7). At the point of the obstruction the streamlines of water flow move away from the bed or wall, leaving a separation, or region of discontinuity of flow. Eddies develop in this region of separation, both upstream and downstream from the obstruction. The actual point of separation and the size and violence of the

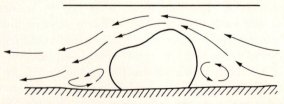

Fig. 3.7 Separation of flow and eddies formed by an obstruction in the channel.

eddies formed depend upon the size of the obstruction and the velocity of the stream.

Matthes proposed a classification of such eddy phenomena (Table 3.2), which he termed macroturbulence. He divided the

Table 3.2 Classification of Eddy Phenomena

Type	Subtype
1. Surge phenomena	*a.* Velocity pulsations
	b. Flood waves
2. Water rollers	*a.* Bank rollers
	b. Bottom rollers
3. Eddies or vortices	*a.* Upward
	b. Downward
4. Helicoidal	

Source: Adapted from Matthes (1947).

types of secondary flow into four different kinds. These secondary movements of water are imposed upon the primary forward flow. Type 1, *surge phenomena,* are rhythmic or cyclic and include velocity pulsations, which seem to be inherent in streamflow, and fluctuations in the level of the water surface. Rise and fall of the water level may be caused by flood crests or by local changes in direction of flow. Type 2 are a number of continuous rotary movements called *water rollers.* These may be *bank rollers,* which have a vertical axis, or *bottom rollers,* with a horizontal axis. Slow bank rollers may form in bays or areas where the channel is excessively wide, whereas fast bank rollers occur where there is some kind of abutment or projection into the stream channel. Slow bottom rollers form at low-water stages where the stream is overly deep, whereas fast bottom rollers occur at high-water stages downstream from a low obstruction or sill extending across the stream. Both kinds of slow rollers are conducive to deposition, and both types of fast rollers cause erosion.

Type 3 movements are *eddies* of local, intermittent, circular motion, often caused by obstructions in the channel bed or walls.

This vortex action may be upward, with a strong suction which entrains bottom material, or it may be downward, or inclined to the direction of flow, which also results in erosion. Secondary flows of type 4 are of the continuous circular motion known as *helical flow*. This occurs when there are a surface movement of water downward and a corresponding movement of bottom water upward. This motion, superimposed on the general downstream flow of water, results in a pattern of movement in which the streamlines of flow look like coiled springs. Such circulation happens in straight as well as sinuous channels and promotes both erosion and deposition.

Thus we see that the flow of water in natural streams is turbulent. The hydrodynamic theory of turbulent flow as outlined attempts to explain the mechanism of stream action, and so it is extremely important for a total understanding of the fluvial processes by which landforms are developed. The basic principles of fluid hydraulics supply a foundation for inquiry into the variables involved in stream action, their magnitude, and the interaction between them.

REFERENCES AND SELECTED READINGS

Chow, Ven Te (1959)   Open-channel hydraulics: McGraw-Hill, New York.
Lane, E. W. (1937)   Stable channels in erodible materials: Trans. Am. Soc. Civil Engrs., vol. 102, pp. 123–194.
Leighley, J. B. (1934)   Turbulence and the transportation of rock debris by streams: Geograph. Rev., vol. 24, pp. 453–464.
Leliavsky, S. (1955)   An introduction to fluvial hydraulics: Constable, London.
Matthes, G. (1947)   Macroturbulence in natural streams: Trans. Am. Geophys. Union, vol. 28, no. 2, pp. 255–261.
Rouse, H. (ed.) (1950)   Engineering hydraulics: Wiley, New York.
Toffaleti, F. B. (1963)   Deep river velocity and sediment profiles and the suspended sand load: Proc. Federal Interagency Sediment. Conf., U.S. Dept. Agr. ARS 970, pp. 207–228.
Tracy, H. J., and C. M. Lester (1961)   Resistance coefficient and velocity distribution in a smooth rectangular channel: U.S. Geol. Surv. Water Supply Paper 1592A.

4

Transportation of the sediment load

A river's ability to work, i.e., to pick up and transport its sediment load, depends upon its energy. It has been estimated that 95 to 97 percent of the energy of a river is converted to heat by inner turbulence and by friction on its channel walls and bed and thus is lost. Hence, only a small part of the energy is left for transportation of the sediment load. Yet movement of debris is an extremely important stream process. Rivers carry material as debris load, in suspension and along the bed of the channel, and in solution. Table 4.1 gives comparative amounts of material carried annually to the sea by some rivers in North America. According to these figures, the Mississippi and Colorado Rivers carry the highest total load per unit area of drainage. And although the Colorado River drains less than one-fifth the area drained by the Mississippi, it carries almost as much load. Those streams flowing into the Hudson Bay basin carry the smallest load per unit area.

The dissolved load

The chemical content of water is not generally visible except in places where so-called mineral or sulfurous waters are present. One can also note the chemical content of water when a residue is left on the bottom or sides of kettles which have gone dry. In many regions the water supply has to be treated, or "softened," to remove some of the undesirable chemicals. The efficacy of chemical erosion, or corrosion, is also shown by the fact that in humid areas limestone is classed as a weakly resistant rock, whereas in arid regions it is one of the most resistant.

It can certainly be seen from Table 4.1 that corrosion is very

Table 4.1   Suspended and Dissolved Loads Carried by North American Rivers

Basin	Area, mi^2	Estim. total load, $tons/(mi^2)(yr)$	% dissolved load	% suspended load
North Atlantic	159,400	169	77	23
South Atlantic	123,900	270	35	65
East Gulf	142,100	261	45	55
West Gulf	315,700	108	33	67
Mississippi River	1,265,000	477	23	77
Laurentian	175,000	117	99	1
Colorado River	230,000	438	12	88
South Pacific	72,700	252	70	30
North Pacific	270,000	120	83	17
Great Basin	223,000	140	64	36
Hudson Bay	62,000	49	57	43

Source: Data from R. B. Dole and H. Stabler, Denudation: U.S. Geol. Surv. Water Supply Paper 234, 1909.

important in reducing the face of the land. Livingstone recently estimated that a total of some 3,905 million metric tons of soluble material is carried annually from the continents by flowing water (Table 4.2). Some streams carry more dissolved matter than they

Table 4.2   Chemical Denudation of the Continents

Continent	Area, 1,000 mi^2	Runoff, 1,000 cfs	Total dissolved salts, ppm
North America	8,172	5,100	142
Europe	4,211	2,796	182
Asia	17,985	12,431	142
Africa	11,500	6,604	121
Australia	2,970	354	59
South America	7,551	8,962	69

Source: Data from Livingstone (1964).

do solid particles. The variability of the amount in solution depends in great part upon the relative contributions of groundwater and surface runoff to stream discharge. If the stream flow is stable, resulting primarily from groundwater flow, concentration of dissolved salts is generally high. However, when surface runoff is the main contributor to flow of the river, the concentration of dissolved salts is usually low (or lower).

Waters which contain acids are especially potent in solvent power. This is true of rivers which flow through swamps, bogs, and marshes, where the decay of vegetation provides a plentiful supply of organic acids. Biological balance also affects the chemical balance of streams. Many organisms, living in river waters, change the concentration of dissolved material by taking it into their systems when alive and releasing it at death. Gorham suggests that the environmental factors which determine the chemical composition of river water are climate, geology, topography, vegetation, and time.

Variability in most of these factors tends to disappear with increasing basin size so that, in general, waters of very large rivers are somewhat similar in chemical content. Figure 4.1 shows the ions present in certain rivers in the United States, ionic constituents being calculated in percentages of the total dissolved material. Bicarbonate, sulfate, and chloride are the predominant negative ions and calcium and sodium the important positive ions. All together, these five ions make up 90 percent or more of the chemical content of most rivers. Silica, potassium, and magnesium, the most abundant of the minor constituents, generally make up less than 5 percent each. Iron, manganese, fluorine, and nitrate ions are usually present in very small amounts. They may, however, be locally important. The striking thing is that percentages of most of the chemical components show only slight variations from large watershed to large watershed.

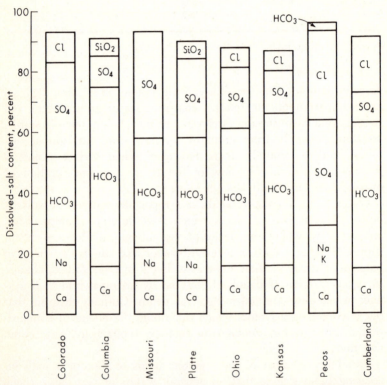

Fig. 4.1 Chemical composition of selected rivers of the United States, mean annual concentration in percent. Major ions are shown for comparison; ions comprising less than 1 percent not shown. Stations at which measurements were taken are as follows: Colorado River at Grand Canyon, Ariz.; Columbia River at Grand Coulee, Wash.; Missouri River at Williston, S.D.; Platte River at Brady, Nebr.; Ohio River at Grand Chain, Ill.; Kansas River at Topeka, Kans.; Pecos River at Red Bluff, N.Mex.; and Cumberland River at Smithland, Ky. (Data from Water Supply Paper 1453.)

However, water in smaller streams often reflects the composition of the surrounding rocks. Table 4.3 shows how the dissolved-salt

Table 4.3 **Dissolved Content of the Ohio River at Four Stations**

Station	SiO₂	Ca	Mg	Na	K	HCO₃	SO₄	Cl	NO₃	Total, ppm
	Mean annual concentration, %									
Cambridge, Pa.*	0.03	0.14	0.05	0.08	0.01	0.07	0.54	0.06	0.02	229
Ravenswood, W.Va.	0.03	0.15	0.03	0.08	0.01	0.16	0.39	0.12	0.01	312
Florence, Ind.	0.02	0.16	0.03	0.07	0.01	0.27	0.33	0.10	0.01	306
Grand Chain, Ill.	0.02	0.16	0.04	0.05	0.01	0.45	0.20	0.07	0.01	186

* The drainage area increases steadily as follows: Cambridge, Pa., 19,560 mi²; Ravenswood, W.Va., 39,840 mi²; Florence, Ind., 82,910 mi²; and Grand Chain, Ill., 203,100 mi².
Source: Data from U.S. Geol. Surv. Water Supply Paper 1452.

content of the Ohio River changes as drainage area increases. In the smallest watershed shown, the sulfate ion is rather high and the bicarbonate rather low. As the basin becomes larger, there is an increase in the percentage of bicarbonate and a corresponding decrease in the sulfate ion. Locally, between Cambridge, Pa., and Florence, Ind., there is an increase in the percent of chloride ion which disappears by the time the water reaches Grand Chain, Ill. On many rivers such as the Ohio, which serve as industrial sites, man's activities may contribute to the chemical content of river water. Certainly, he is to be blamed for the pollutants found there.

The solid-debris load

The solid-debris load, or sediment discharge, of a river is defined as the mass rate of transport through a given cross section, measured as mass per second per foot width. The *solid load* can be divided into the *suspended load* and the *bed load*. The term *wash load* is also used, referring to that part of the sediment load consisting of grains finer than those on the bed of the channel. The bed load is composed of the grains moving along the channel bottom in the lower layers of laminar flow. They move in traction by rolling, sliding, or saltation (jumping) and, in general, are not supported by the fluid.

It is very hard to measure the bed load, or even to estimate it very closely, whereas the suspended load can be measured if care is taken in the procedure. Table 4.4 shows the relation of

Table 4.4 Relation of Suspended Load to Total Load, Boise River Basin

	% of total sediment load	
Location	1939	1940
Boise River near Twin Springs	60–80	50–70
Boise River at Dowling Ranch	50	95–100
Boise River at Notus	80–90	60–80
Moore River above Thorn Creek	95–100	95–100

Source: Data from S. K. Love and P. C. Benedict, Discharge and sediment loads in Boise River drainage basin, Idaho, 1939–1940: U.S. Geol. Surv. Water Supply Paper 1048.

suspended load to total sediment load as estimated at various points along the Boise River. The estimates are very broad, but they show that the proportions of load carried in suspension and in traction differ from time to time and place to place in a given stream.

The bed load

The bed load moves more slowly than the water flows in a stream, since grains move intermittently. The particles may move individually along the bottom, or they may travel in groups. Once in motion, large grains move more easily and faster than small ones, and rounder particles move more easily than flat or angular ones. Grains often move by rolling or sliding and then come to rest before they move again. They will move by saltation if the instantaneous hydrodynamic lift is greater than the weight of the particle, and they will be redeposited wherever the local flow conditions will not reentrain them. Entrainment of grains lying loose on the bed can be caused by: (1) The difference in velocity of adjacent streamlines of flow; i.e., the force exerted by the water on the upper part of the grain is greater than that on the lower part, thus creating a drag or tension. (2) A difference in velocity direction of adjoining filaments of water may cause a similar drag on the grain and entrain it. (3) Upward velocity components or the suction of a rising eddy will also lift a grain from the bottom.

Critical tractive force

The force required to entrain a given grain is called the *critical tractive force,* and the velocity at which this force operates on a given slope is the *erosion velocity*. The relationship between critical drag and grain diameter was investigated by Leliavsky, who compared the results of experiments done in a number of laboratories. Figure 4.2 shows that there is a close correlation, with a regression

$$\tau_c = 166d \tag{4.1}$$

showing that a greater tractive force is needed for entrainment of larger grains. In this equation τ is critical tractive force and d is grain diameter.

The DuBoys equation is generally used to calculate the tractive force in terms of depth of water and stream gradient,

$$\tau = \gamma DS \tag{4.2}$$

where τ is tractive force, γ is specific weight of water, D is depth of water, and S is gradient of the stream. In laboratory experiments, Rubey found that, at low velocities, grains move only if the product

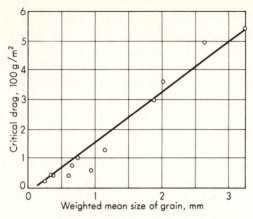

Fig. 4.2 Critical drag shown as a function of grain diameter. Compiled by Leliavsky from results obtained by Engels, Schoklitsch, Gilbert, Schaffernak, Kramer, Krey, and the Prussian Experimental Institute. [Adapted from Leliavsky (1955).]

of depth and slope is great enough. Also, the small grains move at a critical depth-slope product regardless of velocity. Hence, the DuBoys equation expresses the critical tractive force when velocity is low or grains are small. At high velocities, it was found that given grains moved even when depth or slope or both were reduced. So the DuBoys equation does not define the critical tractive force at high velocities. Also, larger particles moved only when a critical velocity was reached, regardless of depth or slope.

In Fig. 4.3 data from various experimenters are compared to determine the effects of depth-slope and velocity on entrainment of grains. This graph supports Rubey's conclusion that the depth-slope product is decisive in initiating movement of small grains, whereas stream velocity is more important for the entrainment of larger particles. Large grains are thought to be subject to the so-called sixth-power law, which states that, for coarse sand and gravel, the size that is moved by traction varies as velocity to the sixth power. However, the exponent should be taken as approximate since it varies with conditions of flow. The largest grain a stream can move as bed load is called its *competence*.

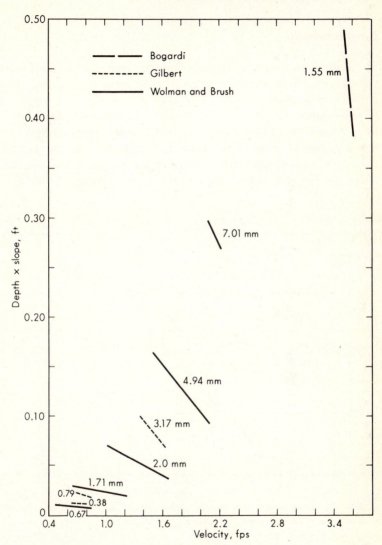

Fig. 4.3 Velocity and depth-slope product required to move particles of a given size. [From Wolman and Brush (1961).]

Erosion velocity

The critical erosion velocity (or competent velocity) is the lowest velocity at which grains of a given size, loose on the bed of a channel, will move. Much lower erosion velocities are required to move sand than to move either silt or gravel. For grains larger than 0.5 mm in diameter, the erosion velocity increases with increasing size of grain. For grains less than 0.5 mm, the erosion velocity increases, but with decreasing size of grain. This is illustrated in Fig. 4.4, where the erosion-velocity curve is shown as

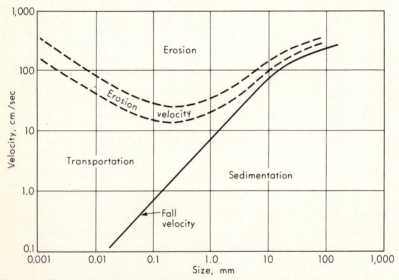

Fig. 4.4 Curves of erosion and deposition for uniform material. Erosion velocity shown as a band. [Redrawn from Hjulstrom (1935).]

a band. A wide area is used to define competent velocity, rather than a line, because the value of erosion velocity varies, depending upon the characteristics of the water and of the grain to be moved.

Grains of the same size, but with different densities, lying on different slopes and with different distributions on the bottom, require different velocities to be moved. Moreover, the erosion velocities vary with depth and density of the water.

The curve of settling velocity, which is shown here as a line, should also be shown as a band of variable settling velocity, again depending upon characteristics of the grain and of the fluid in which the particle is settling. However, these curves suffice to outline broadly the realms of erosion, transportation, and deposition in terms of velocity and size of grains involved. Two important conclusions can be drawn from them. First, we see that sand is easily eroded, whereas silts, clays, and gravels are more resistant. The finer grains are resistant because of strong cohesive forces which bind the grains and because, with smaller grains making up the bottom of the channel, the bed tends to be smooth. There are thus no protruding grains to aid entrainment by forming local eddies or turbulence. Gravel is hard to entrain simply because of the size and weight of the particles. Also, the curves show that, once silts and clays are entrained, they can be transported at much lower velocities. For example, particles 0.01 mm in diameter are entrained at a critical velocity of about 60 cm/sec but remain in motion until the velocity drops even below 0.1 cm/sec.

Settling velocity

Stokes' law of settling velocity applies for small grains. This law follows from an analysis of the forces which are opposing each other and which affect a grain in suspension transport. The resistance a fluid offers a spherical particle falling through it depends on the surface area of the grain, $6\pi r$, viscosity of the fluid, μ, and velocity of fall, V. The buoyant force tending to hold the sphere up in the fluid is equal to the volume of the sphere, $\frac{4}{3}\pi r^2$, times the density of the fluid, d_2, times the force of gravity g. In suspension, this is balanced by the force pulling the grain downward, which equals the volume of the sphere (grain), $\frac{4}{3}\pi r^2$, times its density d_1, times the force of gravity g. We can equate the upward and downward forces for a grain in suspension; so

$$6\pi r\mu V + \tfrac{4}{3}\pi r^3 d_2 g = \tfrac{4}{3}\pi r^3 d_1 g$$

$$6\mu V = \tfrac{4}{3}r^2 g(d_1 - d_2)$$

$$V = \frac{2}{9}\frac{gr^2(d_1 - d_2)}{\mu} \tag{4.3}$$

Hence the rate of settling depends primarily upon grain size and density, since the other factors of gravity, viscosity, and density of water are constant for a given time at a given point in a stream.

However, Stokes' law holds only for small grains which are spherical in shape. For larger grains, the forces of inertia have to be taken into account, and much more complicated formulas apply. In brief, for small grains, settling velocity is proportional to the square of the grain diameter, whereas, for larger particles, settling velocity is proportional to the square root of the grain diameter. Figure 4.5 shows the results of some experimental work on measured fall velocity of sand grains of varying sizes. Velocity of fall increases regularly with grain size to about 0.1 mm, where there is a break in the curve. Above 0.1 mm, fall velocity increases less rapidly with grain diameter. According to this curve, the upward velocity which is needed to keep sand grains in motion changes at a particle size of 0.1 mm. Grains less than 0.1 mm fall with a velocity varying as grain diameter squared; those greater than 0.1 mm in size settle at a velocity which varies as the square root of the diameter. This curve applies only to quartz grains. Empirical data such as these are used to determine rates of settling under particular circumstances to decide, in relation to erosion velocity, whether particles will be transported or deposited. When the upward components of velocity fall below the settling velocity for a given grain size, the particle drops out of suspension and is deposited.

Stream competency and capacity

Competency has already been defined as the largest size of grain that a stream can move in traction as bed load. The competence

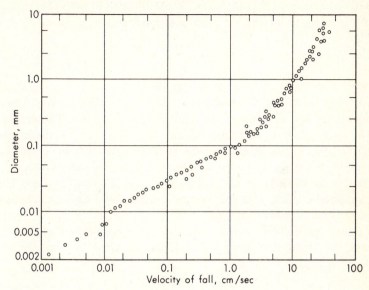

Fig. 4.5 Settling rate of sand (quartz) particles in water. [From Lane (1938).]

of a river changes greatly, not only from head to mouth, but also from time to time at the same spot. A stream can move much larger particles at times of flood when the volume of water and its velocity are high. At such times the competence of a river increases manyfold. It is common to see large boulders lying in the bed of a stream channel, apparently immovable. They were probably carried there by floodwaters, and many years may elapse before another flood occurs strong enough to move them onward.

Capacity, on the other hand, refers to the maximum amount of debris of a given size that a stream can carry in traction as bed load. Gilbert carried on experiments to determine stream capacity under changing conditions of gradient, discharge, and grain size. He changed conditions one at a time, keeping the other variables constant. From the results, he concluded that capacity depends upon stream gradient, discharge, and caliber of load.

As Gilbert held all other factors constant and changed the stream gradient, he found that increasing slope resulted in increased capacity according to the mathematical relationship

$$C = b_1(s - \sigma)^n \qquad (4.4)$$

where C is capacity, s is stream gradient, b_1 and n are empirical constants, and σ is the competent slope, that slope below which the stream has no capacity for material of a given size. The competent slope itself is not independent but is related to discharge, channel width, and fineness of the particles carried. The competent slope varies inversely as the square root of the discharge and must increase as the size of the grains increases. Competent slope has a minimum value at some unique width and increases whether the channel narrows or widens.

Again, as Gilbert varied discharge, keeping other factors constant, he found that increased discharge resulted in increased capacity according to the equation

$$C = b_2(Q - Q_c)^m \qquad (4.5)$$

where C is capacity, b_2 and m are empirical constants, Q is discharge, and Q_c is competent discharge, that discharge below which the stream has no capacity for material of a given size on a given slope. In another experiment, as he changed only the size of the grains carried, Gilbert found that, with increasing grain size, capacity decreased so that

$$C = b_3 \left(\frac{1}{d} + \frac{1}{d_c} \right)^p \qquad (4.6)$$

where C is capacity, b_3 and p are empirical constants, d is the diameter of the grains, and d_c is the size above which the river has no capacity with a given slope and discharge.

Actually the determination of the capacity or actual load of a river is not so simple as these equations make it seem, for all these variables are interrelated and are also affected by stream width, depth, and bed roughness. For example, the fact that there is a much steeper velocity gradient near the bed in a wide, shallow channel (see Fig. 3.3) may be responsible in part for the greater capacity of a channel with this shape. Bed roughness, also, is very important in movement of the bed load because of its influence on turbulence, hydraulic lift, and pressure gradient. Bed roughness, in turn, is related to discharge, to channel morphology and sinuosity, to characteristics of the water such as density and viscosity, to characteristics of the sediment carried, and to the size of bed material.

Another important factor is whether the size of grains in the bed load is varied or homogeneous. Gilbert found that, if fine material were added to the coarse bed load, the total capacity increased as well as the capacity for the coarse material. When he added grains coarser than the particles already in the bed load, total capacity was reduced. The actual change in capacity depends upon the distribution of coarse and fine grains in the mixture and their influence upon bed roughness. If the larger grains are arranged so as to cause local turbulence and eddies, the material is more easily entrained. Larger grains are more easily moved, in turn, on a bed made smooth by small grains. If the large grains are too numerous and too close together, the turbulence they create is not effective, since the eddies interfere with each other. On the other hand, too few large grains become embedded in the fine grains so that they are not moved, nor do they cause enough turbulence to entrain the fine grains.

Regimes of flow

Bedload transport in sand-bed channels depends upon the regime of flow. Streaming flow (page 32) is subcritical and is called the lower- or tranquil-flow regime. Shooting flow is supercritical and is called the upper- or rapid-flow regime. When the Froude number (page 32) is much smaller than 1, flow is tranquil, velocity is low, the water surface is placid, and the channel bottom is rippled. In this regime, resistance to flow is great, and sediment transport is small, with only single grains moving along the bottom. As the Froude number increases but remains less than 1, the form of the bed changes to dunes (Fig. 4.6a). With this configuration,

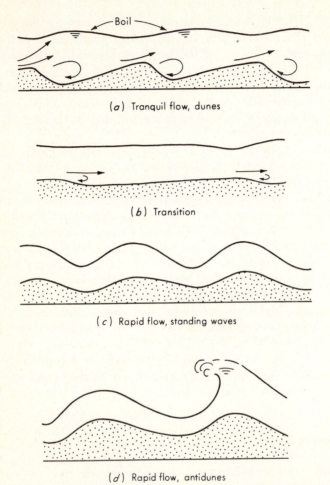

(*a*) Tranquil flow, dunes

(*b*) Transition

(*c*) Rapid flow, standing waves

(*d*) Rapid flow, antidunes

Fig. 4.6 Configuration of channel bottom in loose material under tranquil- and rapid-flow regimes. [Adapted from Simons and Richardson (1960).]

turbulence is generated at the water surface, and eddies form in the lee of the dunes. Group bed movement of grains now takes place, with particles moving up over the back of the dunes and cascading down the steep front. This mass movement causes the dunes to move downstream (Fig. 4.7). When the Froude number becomes larger than 1, flow is rapid, velocity is high, resistance to flow is small, and bed-load transport is great. At the transition to the upper-flow regime the bed form is plane (Fig. 4.6*b*). As the Froude number increases, standing waves form and then anti-

Plate 1　Dunes formed on the outside of a bend of a stream channel during high spring discharge. Bed material was fine and silty, and the dunes disappeared during low flow.

dunes (Fig. 4.6*c* and *d*). Standing waves of water and sand are in phase. Their amplitude and spacing depend upon characteristics of the flow and the bed material. When the amplitude of the water waves increases so that it is greater than the amplitude of the sand waves, antidunes form. These are so-called because, although the sand actually moves downstream, the dunes appear to be moving upstream (Fig. 4.7*b*). This effect is caused by the scour of material from the downstream side of the dune and deposition

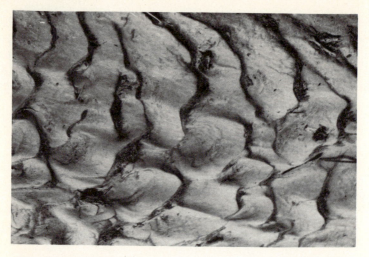

Plate 2 Dunes formed on a fine, silty river bed, completely cover-
ing the channel bottom. Stream near Towaco, N.J.

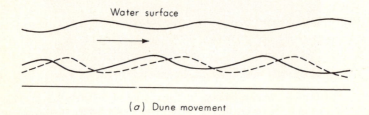

(*a*) Dune movement

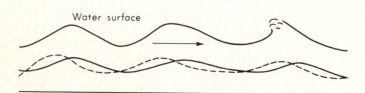

(*b*) Antidune movement

Fig. 4.7 Movement of alluvial-bed material with (*a*) dune and
(*b*) antidune configuration. The dashed lines represent the bottom
after movement of bed material.

on the upstream side. When the water waves have about twice the amplitude of the sand waves, they break and the cycle repeats itself. In the breaking of the waves, turbulence is created, and large quantities of material are carried into suspension by the eddies.

The suspended load

The suspended load is composed of finer particles than the bed load and involves those grains supported by the fluid and carried along above the layer of laminar flow. These particles have settling velocities which are less than the buoyant velocity of the turbulence

Plate 3 Large suspended load brought in by a tributary contrasts with the clear water of the Gauley River, W.Va.

and vortices. Once particles are entrained and part of the suspended sediment load, little or no energy is required to transport them. They can be, and are, carried along by a current which has a velocity less than the critical erosion velocity needed for their entrainment. Moreover, the suspended load decreases the inner turbulence of the water, thus reducing frictional losses of energy and making the stream more efficient.

The distribution of suspended load varies with depth below the surface of the stream. The highest concentration is near the bed and decreases rapidly as one goes higher above the bottom. The actual point of highest concentration depends upon the area of greatest turbulence. For a given grain size, the concentration at any depth below the surface depends upon the settling velocity of the grains and the measure of turbulent mixing.

There is a distinct variation in suspended-sediment concentrations at various depths of a stream for grains of different sizes. Most of the sand grains are carried in suspension near the bottom, as one would expect. There is not very much change in silt concentration with depth, although there may be local changes as a result of eddies. In a study of suspended-sediment concentration in the Mississippi River at Muscatine, Iowa, Lane and Kalinske found that the larger grains tended to be more concentrated near the bottom. For example, sand grains 0.25 to 0.85 mm in diameter decreased steadily from 19.5 parts per million (ppm) near the bed to 0.30 ppm near the surface; grains 0.075 to 0.25 mm in size decreased from 17.1 to 1.1 ppm upward; and grains 0.005 to 0.075 mm in size decreased from 132.7 to 103.3 ppm upward. The silt particles less than 0.005 mm in diameter remained fairly constant throughout the range of depth, from 47.2 ppm at the bottom and varying upward to 46.1 ppm.

A study of the Middle Loup River conducted by Hubbell and Matejka indicated that suspended sediment is more concentrated where velocity is high and depth is low. This conclusion is upheld by flume experiments carried out by Kennedy and Brooks. They found that, with a constant discharge, if depth were held constant and velocity increased, the sediment discharge increased. If discharge and velocity were held constant and depth in the flume increased, sediment discharge decreased. Moreover, there was an increase in sediment-discharge concentration with a change in bed configuration from dune to plane to antidune. Figure 4.8 indicates that, for low velocities and high depths, at constant discharge and with a dune bed form, sediment discharge is low. At high velocities and low depth, with constant discharge and a flat bed configuration, sediment discharge is high. With high velocities and an antidune state, sediment transport continues to increase.

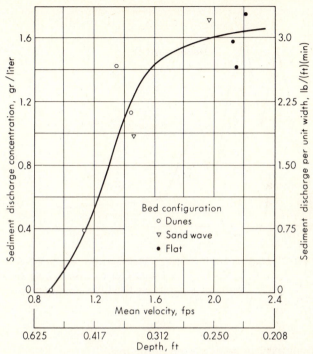

Fig. 4.8 Variation of sediment-discharge concentration and sediment-transport rate with mean velocity and depth, for a constant discharge of 0.50 cfs/ft. [After Kennedy and Brooks (1963).]

Suspended load and discharge

Observations show a fairly good correlation between suspended load and stream discharge. Figure 4.9 shows the average annual discharge and average suspended load carried yearly by the Colorado River at the Grand Canyon gaging station. This shows a very good correlation of suspended-sediment discharge with flow of water until about 1934. The disparity after that is a result of damming. This kind of regular relationship permits the determination of a sediment-discharge rating curve for a particular river. Such curves form a straight line when plotted on logarithmic scales.

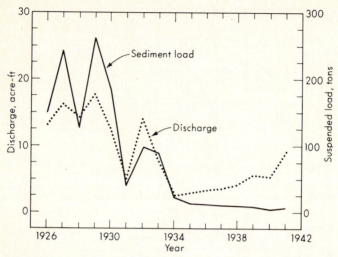

Fig. 4.9 Average annual discharge and average suspended load carried by the Colorado River at Grand Canyon, Ariz. (Data from C. S. Howards, Suspended sediment in the Colorado River, 1925–1941: Water Supply Paper 998.

The relationship can be expressed in the form

$$M = kQ^n \tag{4.7}$$

where M is rate of sediment movement, Q is discharge, and k and n are empirical constants which differ from river to river. Figure 4.10 is the sediment rating curve for the Rio Puerco River. It allows prediction, within limits of the curve, of sediment load with a given discharge.

The change in concentration of suspended load was measured for the Enoree River as discharge changed during a flood (Fig. 4.11). The graph shows that the amount of suspended-sediment load increased more quickly than the flood discharge and reached a peak concentration some 6 hr before the floodwaters did. The suspended load carried during the highest water flow was thus considerably less than capacity. This has also been shown to be true for other rivers.

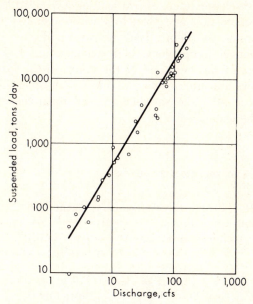

Fig. 4.10 Sediment rating curve for the Rio Puerco River near Cabezon, N.Mex. [From Leopold and Maddock (1955).]

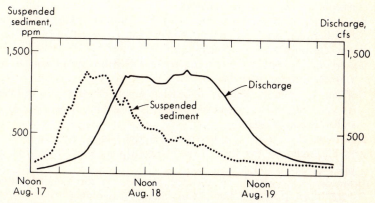

Fig. 4.11 Suspended-sediment load and flood discharge for the Enoree River, S.C., Aug. 17–19, 1939. [From Einstein, Anderson, and Johnson (1940).]

Sediment discharge, then, as bed load or suspended load, is variable from time to time and place to place in a stream. The factors which determine the debris load are stream discharge, velocity, gradient, channel morphology, bed roughness, and the physical characteristics of the fluid and of the grains in the load. In turn, these variables are interrelated and affect each other. Over a long period of time all these variables depend upon the climate and geology of the watershed.

REFERENCES AND SELECTED READINGS

Brooks, N. H. (1963) Calculation of sediment load discharge from velocity and concentration parameters: Proc. Federal Interagency Sediment. Conf., U.S. Dept. Agr. ARS 970, pp. 229–237.

Chow, Ven Te (1959) Open-channel hydraulics: McGraw-Hill, New York.

Colby, B. R. (1961) Effect of depth of flow on discharge of bed material: U.S. Geol. Surv. Water Supply Paper 1498D.

——— (1964) Discharge of sands and mean velocity relationships in sand-bed streams: U.S. Geol. Surv. Prof. Paper 462A.

Douglas, I. (1964) Intensity and periodicity in denudation with special reference to the removal of material in solution by rivers: Z. Geomorph., vol. 8, no. 4, pp. 453–473.

Einstein, H. A., A. G. Anderson, and J. W. Johnson (1940) A distinction between bed load and suspended load in natural streams: Trans. Am. Geophys. Union, pp. 628–632.

Gilbert, G. K. (1914) The transportation of debris by running water: U.S. Geol. Surv. Prof. Paper 86.

Gorham, E. (1961) Factors influencing supply of major ions to inland waters, with special reference to the atmosphere: Geol. Soc. Amer. Bull. 72, pp. 795–840.

Hjulstrom, F. (1935) Studies of the morphological activity of rivers as illustrated by the River Fyris: Univ. Upsala Geol. Inst. Bull. 25, pp. 221–527.

Howards, C. S. (1947) Suspended sediment in the Colorado River, 1925–1941: U.S. Geol. Surv. Water Supply Paper 998.

Hubbell, D. W., and D. Q. Matejka (1959) Investigations of sediment transport, Middle Loup River at Dunning, Neb.: U.S. Geol. Surv. Water Supply Paper 1476.

Kennedy, J. F., and N. H. Brooks (1963) Laboratory study of an alluvial stream at constant discharge: Proc. Federal Interagency Sediment. Conf., U.S. Dept. Agr. ARS 970, pp. 320–329.

Lane, E. W. (1938) Notes on formation of sand: Trans. Am. Geophys. Union, vol. 18, pp. 505–508.

—— and W. M. Borland (1954) River bed scour during floods: Trans. Am. Soc. Civil Engrs., vol. 119, pp. 1069–1080.

—— and A. A. Kalinske (1941) Engineering calculations of suspended sediment: Trans. Am. Geophys. Union, no. 22, pp. 603–607.

Leliavsky, S. (1955) An introduction to fluvial hydraulics: Constable, London.

Leopold, L. B., and T. Maddock (1955) The hydraulic geometry of stream channels and some physiographic implications: U.S. Geol. Surv. Prof. Paper 252.

—— and J. P. Miller (1956) Ephemeral streams: hydraulic factors and their relation to the drainage net: U.S. Geol. Surv. Prof. Paper 282A.

Livingstone, D. A. (1964) Chemical composition of rivers and lakes: U.S. Geol. Surv. Prof. Paper 440G.

Menard, H. W. (1950) Sediment movement in relation to current velocity: Jour. Sediment. Petrol., vol. 20, pp. 148–160.

Nordin, C. F., Jr., and G. R. Dempster, Jr. (1963) Vertical distribution of velocity and suspended sediment, Middle Rio Grande, N. Mexico; U.S. Geol. Surv. Prof. Paper 462B.

Rubey, W. (1933) Equilibrium conditions in debris-laden streams: Trans. Amer. Geophys. Union, vol. 14, pp. 497–505.

Simons, D. B., and E. V. Richardson (1960) The effect of bed roughness on depth-discharge relations in alluvial channels: U.S. Geol. Surv. Water Supply Paper 1498E.

U.S. Geol. Surv. Water Supply Paper 1453 (1960) Quality of surface waters of the United States, 1956, parts 9–14.

Wolman, M. G., and L. M. Brush, Jr. (1961) Factors controlling the size and shape of stream channels in coarse noncohesive sands: U.S. Geol. Surv. Prof. Paper 282G.

5

The fluvial processes: erosion

The total work of a stream is measured by the amount of material it erodes, transports, and deposits. Dole and Stabler estimated that the surface of the United States is being removed at the rate of 1 in. in 760 years, or 0.0013 in./year. Of this, approximately one-third is removed as dissolved matter and two-thirds as suspended load. They stated that 270 million tons of dissolved material and 513 million tons of solid material reach the ocean yearly. Their figures led to the approximate rate of denudation for the United States of 1 ft in 10,000 years which has been generally accepted.

Erosional processes

Erosion is carried on by rivers through the processes of corrosion, corrasion, and cavitation. Any chemical process which results from

Plate 4   Large rocks, smoothed by river abrasion, lie in the channel of Johns Brook, in the Adirondack Mountains, N.Y. (Photograph courtesy of G. Dougherty.)

the reaction of water and rocks on the surface of the land is classed as *corrosion. Corrasion* is the mechanical wearing away of land, generally by the impact or grinding action of particles carried by the stream. Abrasion of the surface over which water flows is shown by the smooth polishing of rocks in a bedrock channel. A particular kind of corrasion is *evorsion*, which results from the sheer force of water on bedrock, without tools. Potholes may be formed by evorsion. *Hydraulicking* is the removal of loose material by the force of impact of water alone. This type of erosion occurs often in alluvial channels.

The third process, *cavitation*, occurs under very high velocities only. A theorem of Bernoulli states that the total energy of a stream is constant. The potential energy can be expressed as the pressure

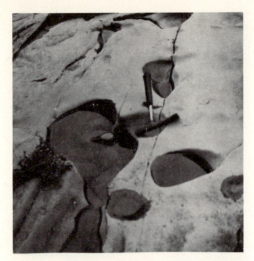

Plate 5   Smoothed bedrock surface with potholes in the channel of Birch Creek, Glen
Helen, Ohio.

head due to the weight of water and elevation difference,

$$E_p = \frac{P}{\gamma} + z \qquad (5.1)$$

where P is pressure, z is difference in elevation (head), and γ is specific weight of water. Kinetic energy can be expressed as

$$E_k = \rho \frac{V^2}{2} \qquad (5.2)$$

where V is velocity and ρ is density. So total stream energy can be equated as

$$E_t = \rho \frac{V^2}{2} + \frac{P}{\gamma} + z = \text{a constant} \qquad (5.3)$$

Thus, a constriction in the channel which will cause an increase in stream velocity will also raise the kinetic-energy term. Since γ, ρ, z, and total energy remain the same, pressure must decrease to keep the equation in balance. If the pressure decreases to the vapor pressure of water, bubbles will form. Then, with a subsequent widening of the channel and decrease in velocity, the opposite reaction occurs; pressure increases, which causes the bubbles to collapse, giving off shock waves. These travel outward to the channel walls and result in very strong stresses, rather like the blows of a hammer, which cause rapid erosion. However, cavitation is rare because of the very high velocities required. It seems to occur only in waterfalls, rapids, and some artificial conduits.

The hydraulicking, abrasive, and cavitation effects of flowing water are aided in erosion by the sucking, lifting forces of vortex action as demonstrated in Fig. 5.1. Loose grains are sucked upward

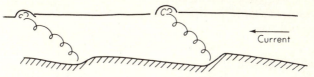

Fig. 5.1 Vortex action in lee of dunes, which causes entrainment of loose particles. [After Matthes (1947).]

and downstream with the vortex current. Also, during ordinary flow streamlines of water are diverted and their velocities changed when they encounter obstacles in the bed or impinge on channel walls or meander bends. A discontinuity or separation of flow occurs where there is such a local change in direction or in velocity, resulting in a nonuniform distribution of energy at that point. Thus there is a veering and overturning of water masses as spiral flow. The amount of separation, turbulence, and vortex action depends upon the velocity of the water, the size of the obstruction, the spacing of obstacles (if there is more than one), and the sharpness of the river bend. Separation of flow can result in deposition where velocity is decelerated. However, the erosive effects can be seen in Fig. 5.2. The force of the eddies results in erosion of the boulder, as well as the channel bed. Where an eddy is formed by the upward surge of water at the sides of a channel, the vortex has a swirling, lifting force which acts to carve a hole on the bottom. Such whirling eddies cause both abrasion in bedrock and entrain-

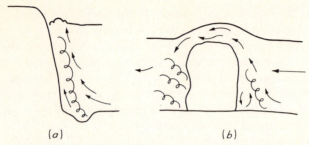

Fig. 5.2 Erosive effects of vortices (*a*) along a channel wall where there is an upsurge of water and (*b*) where a large boulder lies in a stream bed. [After Matthes (1947).]

ment of loose particles. The vortex action at a meander bend causes the meander to move progressively downstream.

Channel development

Any rain falling on the earth's surface which does not sink into the ground runs downhill in response to the force of gravity. Even a "level" surface is never really flat but contains minor irregularities with shallow areas into which water can run. At first the rain may run off as overland flow in an unconcentrated sheet wash. But soon rills form, channeling the flow into shoestring gullies. These shoestring gullies, in turn, increase in width, depth, and length, forming larger channelways. Or, because of the underlying rock type and structure, channeling may develop immediately without rill formation. Large gullies sometimes are cut into bare hillslopes during a single, extremely intense and heavy rainstorm. Morisawa found that, on flat ground surfaces composed of fine-grained material without a vegetative cover, rainstorms produced sizable channels which followed mud-crack patterns formed during dry periods.

Channels and gullies grow headward, thus increasing their length. Headward erosion results generally from undercutting at the base, especially where the surface is protected by a resistant stratum, soil or vegetation. The undercutting may be caused by

Plate 6 Headward erosion of a small tributary will soon divert the water of the main channel, leaving an erosion remnant or miniature butte. Near Buena Vista, Colo.

groundwater percolation which removes the underlying fine material. Sometimes rather large underground pipes or tunnels can be formed in this way. These may be later exposed by infall at the head, or upstream, and become part of the gully channelway. The author has seen discontinuous gullies in the Appalachian Plateau which were probably formed in this way.

Or, again, the flow of water under the surface may simply moisten or loosen the soil under the protective cover, causing it to fall or to be easily removed. Once the head is undercut, gravity causes the upper, resistant layer to fall. Another way in which gullies may be eroded headward is by plunge-pool action during excessive storms. Many gully heads have been observed to be stationary for long periods of time, extending themselves headward only at periods of intense rainfall.

Channel widening

Streams widen their channels in a number of ways. They may do this by vigorous lateral corrasion against the walls during flood-times or when a meander bend impinges against the valley sides. A channel may also be shifted laterally when streamlines of flow are deflected by boulders or debris in it. Erosion is also caused on channel sidewalls owing to diversion brought about by the load or from the impetus of water itself brought in by a tributary. Much valley widening occurs as a result of weathering and mass movements on the valley sides as the stream cuts downward. Much debris creeps, slumps, slides, or falls into the channel floor, where it is removed periodically by the stream. Or weathered material, loose on the valley side slopes, may be removed by rainwash or by flash floods in the channel.

Perhaps one of the most spectacular examples of valley widening is the Grand Canyon of the Colorado. Here the river has carved a path some 4,000 ft deep with a valley about 6 miles wide. Since the stream has cut through a series of essentially flat-lying, alternating hard and soft rock, its walls form a *cliff and slope* type of topography. That is, the resistant layers of sandstone, conglomerate, and limestone form flat benches or terraces, while the less resistant shale beds form slopes as in Fig. 5.3. The Tonto platform of the

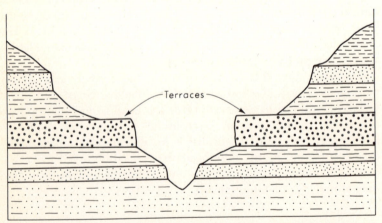

Fig. 5.3 Diagram of cliff and slope topography with rock terraces or benches formed on resistant strata. Such topography is common in regions of dissection on flat-lying sediments and is most evident in arid or semiarid regions.

Canyon is such a structural terrace, formed on resistant Tapeats sandstone. Widening and retreat of the canyon walls occur mostly by sliding and other kinds of mass movements, but it is the river which has been ever cutting downward.

In regions of massive resistant rock where retreat of the sidewalls has been much slower than valley deepening, steep and narrow canyons result. Valley deepening as well as widening takes place during peak discharges, when both volume of water and volume of load are greatest. Irregular longitudinal downcutting is characteristic of streams and is manifested in almost all natural channels in bedrock, and even on a minute scale in alluvial channels. This results from changes in flow characteristics or from changes in channel-bed material.

Valley shape

Some valleys are cut so that they are narrow and V-shaped in cross section, while others are steep-walled and somewhat U-shaped. The traditional view has been that such shapes are characteristic of the stage of the erosion cycle of the stream. Hence,

Plate 7   V-shaped gorge of the Blackwater River, W.Va., exemplifies the classic shape of the youthful stream valley.

a V-shaped valley was taken to mean a stream in *youth*, while a valley which was broad, wide-bottomed, and steep-walled was *mature* or *old*. However, rather than indicating a stage of erosion, valley shape is often the result of the interaction of climate, available relief, rock type, and geologic structure. Climate directly influences both the volume of flow in a stream and vegetative cover on the surface. Vegetation partly controls the amount of runoff, as well as supplying a protective cover to the surface. Its effect is such that in extremely rainy, tropical areas stream valleys are deep and narrow because the dense vegetation prohibits wall erosion. In temperate, moist regions sidewalls are smoothed to a gentler slope by creep and soil wash, giving a typical V-shaped valley. On the other hand, in arid regions where the ground surface is bare and exposed, stream valleys are often steep-walled and flat-bottomed, resulting in a U shape.

Available relief is important because it plays a part in determining the ratio of downcutting to sidecutting in a stream valley. The rock type influences the shape of a stream valley and channel, since it partly determines the amount of runoff and the resistance of the surface to erosion. In a study of some newly formed stream channels on recently upraised and exposed lake beds, Morisawa found that valleys cut in unconsolidated beach sands and gravels were V-shaped, while those cut into silts and muds were flat-bottomed and steep-walled. The loose, sandy material tended to fall from the valley sides, giving it a V-shaped aspect, with wall slopes at the angle of repose of the sand. Rain, falling on such porous material, sinks into the bed and ground surface, thus maintaining the valley shape rather than clearing the channel. Sidewalls in the finer-grained material maintain their steepness because of the cohesiveness of silts and clays. Infall to the valley bottom, occurring as blocks of material, leaves the walls vertical. It must be kept in mind that these valleys were miniature, though real, in the beginning stage of erosion and that the ground surface was unvegetated.

Stream terraces

Another landform resulting from stream erosion is the alluvial terrace, formed when a river cuts into the floodplain which it had previously deposited. The terrace consists of a flat area or bench cut off by a scarp (Fig. 5.4). The terrace lies some distance above the elevation of the present stream so that the river no longer flows on it, even during times of flood. It may or may not extend along both sides of the stream valley. If terraces do exist along both sides of the valley and at the same elevation, they are called *paired terraces*.

The terrace may be formed of bedrock, in which case it is called

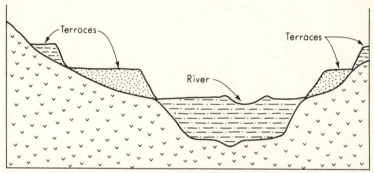

Fig. 5.4 Sketch of a valley filled with alluvium which has been eroded into terraces. Each terrace is coded by a pattern.

Plate 8 An ephemeral stream, its sinuous course incised into flat-lying bedrock terraces, flows across the plains of Kansas.

a *strath terrace,* or it may be formed on alluvium. In the latter case, the stream had previously cut a wide channel in the bedrock and partly filled it with floodplain deposits. Then some change in the environment caused the river to erode its former deposits. The change may have been tectonic; i.e., the area may have been uplifted or tilted. The change may have been a climatic one which influenced the stream's discharge or sediment load. Or the water-

Plate 9   A tributary incises its channel into the floodplain of the main stream. Near Buena Vista, Colo.

shed environment may have been changed by man himself. Often the environment of a stream may be changed a number of times, as demonstrated by a series of terraces, each at a different level. The river pictured in Fig. 5.4 has several terraces at different elevations.

Terraces are often used as guides in interpreting the geologic history of a region. In unstable regions of the world, such as Japan, terraces are usually a result of tectonic uplift. In many places they are caused by our most recent change in climate, from glacial to interglacial. River valleys which had been deeply and widely cut by glacial ice and/or meltwater filled these with thick deposits as they carried debris from the dwindling glaciers. A combination of changing climate and discharge and postglacial rebound brought about incision into these deposits, forming terraces as the stream cut a new channel.

Plate 10   Several upraised floodplain terraces of the Madison River near Ennis, Mont.

Factors influencing soil erosion

A stream valley, then, is one of the visible effects of erosion by running water, whether the valley be a tiny shoestring gully or a Grand Canyon. The actual amount of erosion depends primarily upon the climate and the physical and geological characteristics of the land surface. Langbein and Schumm hold that the most important factor is effective precipitation, i.e., precipitation adjusted to that yielding equivalent runoff in regions having a mean annual temperature of 50°F. These men gathered data on sediment yield in small drainage basins in the United States and concluded that stream erosion in these watersheds averaged 0.10 to 0.34 ft/1,000 years (Table 5.1). The slowest denudation rates by stream action occurred when precipitation was very high, because of protection by vegetation. Stream denudation was greatest where effective rainfall was too low to promote vegetative cover but high enough to provide excess runoff. This occurs in regions with approximately 10 to 15 in./year of rainfall. Rates of erosion fall off on both sides of this maximum, either because of rainfall deficiency or because of increased density of vegetation.

Table 5.1   Rates of Stream Denudation

| Effective precipitation, in. | Measured mean sediment yield, tons/mi² | Estimated mean denudation | |
		ft/1,000 yr	yr/ft
10	670	0.29	3,400
10–15	780	0.34	2,900
15–20	550	0.24	4,200
20–30	550	0.24	4,200
30–40	400	0.17	5,900
40–60	220	0.10	10,000

Source: Stream data on the average from areas 1,500 square miles, taken from S. A. Schumm, The disparity between present rates of denudation and orogeny: U.S. Geol. Surv. Prof. Paper 454H, 1963.

Rates of erosion are also determined by geologic factors such as rock and soil type and characteristics, as well as the topographic factors of surface slope, orientation, elevation, and relief. Figure 5.5 is a simplified and diagrammatic flow chart of the action, inter-action, and feedback of the factors which influence the rate of erosion. Climate and geology are taken as the broad, long-term

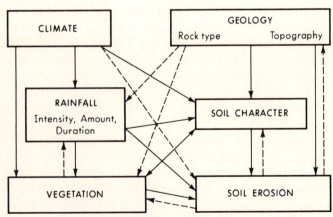

Fig. 5.5   Flow chart of the factors which influence soil erosion.

independent variables. Factors of rainfall, soil character, and vegetation are dependent upon the climate and geology and are also interrelated to each other. All these influence not only the amount and rates of erosion but also the size and shape of the landscape created by the stream.

REFERENCES AND SELECTED READINGS

Dole, R. B., and H. Stabler (1909) Denudation: U.S. Geol. Surv. Water Supply Paper 234, pp. 78–93.

Guy, H. P. (1964) An analysis of some storm-period variables affecting stream sediment transport: U.S. Geol. Surv. Prof. Paper 462E.

Langbein, W. B., and S. A. Schumm (1958) Yield of sediment in relation to mean annual precipitation: Trans. Am. Geophys. Union, vol. 39, pp. 1076–1084.

Matthes, G. (1947) Macroturbulence in natural streams: Trans. Am. Geophys. Union, vol. 28, no. 2, pp. 255–261.

Menard, H. W. (1961) Some rates of regional erosion: Jour. Geol., vol. 69, no. 2, pp. 154–161.

Morisawa, M. E. (1964) Development of drainage systems on an upraised lake floor: Am. Jour. Sci., vol. 262, pp. 340–354.

Schumm, S. A. (1961) Effect of sediment characteristics on erosion and deposition in ephemeral stream channels: U.S. Geol. Surv. Prof. Paper 352C.

——— (1963) The disparity between present rates of denudation and orogeny: U.S. Geol. Surv. Prof. Paper 454H.

——— and R. F. Hadley (1957) Arroyos and the semi-arid cycle of erosion: Am. Jour. Sci., vol. 255, pp. 161–174.

Sundborg, A. (1956) The river Klarälven, a study of fluvial processes: Geograph. Ann., vol. 38, pp. 127–316.

6

The fluvial processes: deposition

Another visible result of stream erosion is the landforms created by stream deposition. Sedimentation of the particles picked up and carried away by rivers results in braided streams, alluvial floodplains, deltas, fans, and bahadas. Braided streams have a complex maze of channels which thread their way among bars deposited on the river bottom. They will be discussed in detail in a later chapter.

Particles entrained and transported by a river are deposited when the current is no longer competent to carry them. *Competence* may be said to result from an excess of stream velocity over and above the setting velocity of the grains in transport. It varies at different times and at different points in the flow of water in the same stream.

Loss of transporting ability

As we have seen, there are many factors which tend to modify or lessen the transporting ability of a stream. A loss of capacity and/or competence may be caused by decreased gradient, decreased volume, increased caliber of load, or damming of the channel, for instance. A stream gradient may change when the stream flows from one rock type to another. Furthermore, an increase in stream length with the same vertical fall, as in a meander, will result in a gradient which is gentler. Gradient is suddenly decreased when a stream debouches from a steep mountain front onto a plain or when it moves into a still body of water. In all these cases, a decrease in gradient causes a loss of transporting ability and deposition of the load.

Decreased volume may occur when an increase in vegetative cover promotes infiltration and detention of rainwater through storage and vegetative use. It may also occur from a change in climate whereby less rain is supplied to a stream. In arid regions, volume of water decreases downstream as the river loses water by evaporation or seepage. Decrease in volume may also occur if a river is naturally diverted by another stream in an act of piracy or if it is artificially diverted by man. Again, loss of competence and deposition of the load will occur as a result of this decrease in discharge.

Deposition may also occur when the load supplied to a stream exceeds its competency or capacity. Excessive load is often provided from glacial outwash or accelerated erosion of a denuded watershed. Often a steeper, more turbulently flowing tributary bears boulders which the main stream is incompetent to carry, and so these are deposited at the junction. Change in caliber of load may also cause deposition, when grain size is increased beyond the competency. This may happen when a stream which is incising its own floodplain encounters material of a larger grain size. It may be competent to entrain and carry the particles away at the point of encounter but may be incompetent further downstream and may thus deposit the particles.

Alluvial floodplains

An alluvial floodplain is the most common depositional feature of streams. It is not limited to large rivers, as is commonly thought;

even a small brook may have a floodplain. The alluvium is made up of many kinds of deposits, laid down both in the channel and outside it. To account for these deposits, let us look at the stream in hydrodynamic terms. In order to obtain the equation of continuity (Chap. 3), we assumed that the flow of water in a river channel was steady and uniform. That is, we assumed that depth did not vary with time at a given point along the channel and that depth did not vary at any one given instant of time along the length of the channel. Let us now consider what happens if the flow is steady but nonuniform. That is, we now assume that depth does vary at different places along the length of the stream. Then, where changing conditions of depth occur, there will be local accelerations and decelerations in the stream flow.

Based on this idea, Leliavsky attributes erosion to convergent streamlines of flow and deposition to divergent streamlines. Where masses of water are moving so that they converge, the resulting acceleration of velocity increases ability to transport and particles are entrained. Where there is a movement of water so that masses diverge or spread out, they are decelerated. The loss of velocity means a local loss of ability to transport, and particles are dropped. This idea has recently been supported by Wertz, who, after studying channel scour and fill in some arroyos in the southwestern United States, stated that the location of patchy sand deposits depended upon lateral and vertical changes in velocity. Local accelerations and decelerations of stream flow resulted from outcrops and trees along the channel, as well as from confluences with tributaries and meander bends.

Certainly, variation in transverse distribution of flow velocity (see Fig. 3.3) should result in changing ability to transport at various points in the cross section of a stream. Variation in turbulence at different points should also have an effect upon capacity and competence. Thus, Leighley explains erosion and deposition in terms of regions of maximum and minimum turbulence (see Fig. 3.6). Deposition occurs where turbulence is at a minimum or where the region of turbulence is high above the bottom. Observation shows that greater turbulence at one point leads to scour, while a lessening of turbulence results in deposition. In particular, one type of turbulence is that caused by helical flow. This rotary

current leads to turbulence, plus a downward, converging movement of water on the outside of a meander bend, where erosion
takes place (Fig. 6.1). On the inner side of the bend, the rotary
motion is upward, with a deceleration and lessening of turbulence,
causing deposition. Thus, lateral accretion occurs with deposition
of a point bar on the inside of a meander bend (Fig. 6.1). It

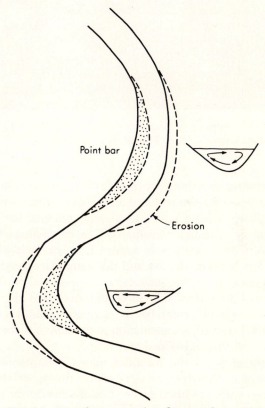

Point bar

Erosion

Fig. 6.1 Meandering stretch indicating the position
of growth of point bars on the inner side of a bend
and erosion on the outer edge. Transverse profiles at
the bends show the asymmetry resulting from the
erosion and deposition accentuated or brought on by
the lateral movement of water masses.

Plate 11   Beginning of point-bar deposits along the inner part of a stream meander. Near Towaco, N.J.

is formed downstream from the point of greatest curvature of the bend and is generally composed of a mixture of grain sizes. According to Sundborg, a point bar starts as a longitudinal bar extending from the tip of a meander headland. The longitudinal bar grows downstream, with its steep side toward the shore and with a long narrow trough between the bar and the shore. As vegetation grows on this exposed bar, other material is trapped and builds up the sediment until the steep side faces the river and the trough is filled in. Whereas the point bar is composed mainly of material carried in the bed load, sedimentation in the trough is accomplished by deposition of suspended-load material.

Point bars grow as the meander moves downstream, or new ones are built as the river changes course during or after floods. Old meander scars can often be seen on the floodplain (Fig. 6.2). These are formed when the meander is cut off, becomes a slough or an oxbow lake, and is eventually filled with sediment. This combination of point bar and filled slough results in what is called *ridge and swale* topography. The ridges are composed of sandbars

Plate 12   Fully developed point bar, showing inner channel. The profile shows a buildup on the inside and an outer sloping edge. Catskill Creek, N.Y.

Plate 13   Meander scars on a floodplain near Coshocton, Ohio.

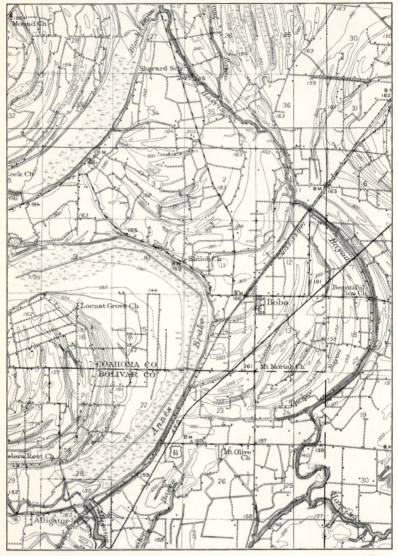

Fig. 6.2   Part of the Clarksdale, Miss., quadrangle, showing some old meander scars on the floodplain of the Mississippi River. Concentric ridges show point bars, and sloughs and swamps indicate old channels.

and the swales are the depressions filled with silt-clay slough deposits.

Vertical accretion, or the building up of a floodplain, is accomplished by inchannel and overbank deposits, during and immediately after floods. As the river overtops its channel banks and spreads out, its ability to transport material is lessened. Thus some of the coarser particles are dropped near the edge of the channel and, if they remain there, may build up a natural levee. Finer material is carried farther from the channel and laid down as back-swamp deposits. As the floodwaters recede, more material is deposited in these areas as well as in the channel itself. Thus, it is commonly thought that both the river bed and its floodplain are built upward by sedimentation during and right after peak flows. Figure 6.3 shows a map of these various kinds of deposits comprising the floodplain of a part of the Mississippi River, with prominent ridge and swale topography.

In a study of the Cimarron River in southwestern Kansas, Schumm and Lichty found that, when a period of drought allowed sparse vegetation on the floodplain other than grass, the large floods which occurred destroyed the floodplain by erosion. However, when abundant rains promoted the growth of brush and trees and there were no large floods, the floodplain was built up by sedimentation. Thus, they attribute floodplain growth to the establishment of vegetation, which not only prevents erosion but stabilizes the floodplain and aids deposition. It has already been pointed out that point bars also are stabilized and their troughs filled in when vegetal growth helps in trapping sediment.

Schumm and Lichty also determined that the new floodplain was constructed predominantly by vertical accretion, as bars and islands coalesced, and by overbank deposition. Channel areas favorable for construction of the floodplain were found to be at the crests of meander bends and in the lee of these bends, at the junction of tributaries, in abandoned and low-water channels, and where some islands had already formed. Later meandering by the stream over these floodplain deposits caused reworking of the sediments. They point out that such an occurrence may lead to a misconception that the floodplain was originally formed by lateral accretion.

Plate 14   Point bars developed along the North Branch of the South Platte River near Fairplay, Colo.

Lattman found five basic types of deposits in the floodplain of Beaverdam Run, Pa. They were colluvium, lag deposits, channel fill, deposits of lateral accretion, and deposits of vertical accretion. The colluvium consisted of angular chunks of bedrock in a clay matrix. This debris had evidently slumped or slid from the valley sides. The colluvium also contained interbedded layers of alluvium. The lag deposits were discontinuous and represented coarse debris which had been laid down in the channel bottom and from which finer material had been washed away. The channel fill was well-rounded and poorly sorted silt, sand, and gravel. Although others have stated that deposits of lateral accretion are not necessarily composed of coarser grains than overbank material, Lattman found he could distinguish between these two types of material on the basis of grain size. In Beaverdam Run, the deposits of lateral accretion were predominantly sand, with some silt and gravel. Overbank deposits were clay and silt, with only a small amount of sand. It seems logical that the sizes of grains in deposits of vertical and lateral accretion should vary from stream to stream. In fact, such deposits would probably vary from point to point along the same stream.

The Mississippi River floodplain

The floodplain of the Mississippi River is one of the largest and most striking and has been thoroughly investigated and mapped. Fisk made a detailed study of it and divided its deposits into two large categories on the basis of grain size, graveliferous and nongraveliferous deposits. The graveliferous section comprises about 25 percent of the alluvium of the Mississippi valley. Actually, however, the gravel is disseminated throughout a sand matrix. The section is composed of deposits of the type formed by braided rivers, with sands and gravels interfingering and overlapping each other. There is a basal unit which grades upward into finer deposits of sand, silt, and clay, which form the nongraveliferous section. This upper unit has a basal pervious sand, partly overlain and partly interfingered with impervious silt and clay strata. The sands themselves are large, discontinuous, irregularly shaped lenses. They thin out along the edges of the valley and to the south and north, having their greatest thickness in the central portion of the floodplain. These deposits are a combination of natural levee sediments, sandbar ridges, channel and slough fillings, and backswamp deposits (Fig. 6.3). Natural levee sediments are ridgelike masses of silty materials which thin and become finer away from the channel edges. They are thickest on the outside of bends and are widest where the stream channel itself is widest. Sandbar ridges are caused by shifting of the channel or by accretion on the concave side of river bends, where the current slackens. These sand lenses are covered with silt which is laid down during flood stages. Channel and slough fillings are generally clay plugs and result from sedimentation of fine-grained material in old channels, troughs, or sloughs between bars or cutoffs. Fisk distinguishes between neck- and chute-type cutoffs. The neck type is formed by coalescence of bends. When the neck is narrow enough, the water breaks through and forms a cutoff. This kind of cutoff is rapidly abandoned by the stream, forms an oxbow lake, and is rapidly silted up. A chute-type cutoff is formed when the river takes a new course across a point bar on the inside of a bend. The old channel

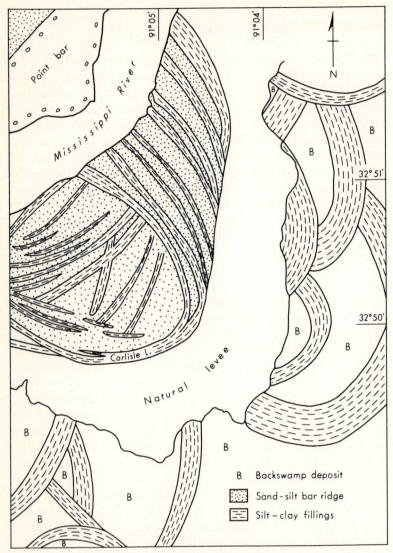

Fig. 6.3 Map of a portion of the Mississippi River floodplain, showing various kinds of deposits. [From Fisk (1944).]

is abandoned slowly and, with the gradual reduction in flow, is filled with silty-sand material and finally with clay. Backswamp deposits are the most widespread feature of the top stratum which covers the flood basin and thickens to the south. It is high in organic content and is composed mainly of silt, thinly interbedded with clay. On the south this vast floodplain merges with the Mississippi delta deposits.

The former bedrock valley is rugged (Fig. 6.4) and filled with the alluvium just described, approximately 1,000 cubic miles in volume. The deposits are all fairly young, sedimentation occurring during the last glacial epoch. The present floodplain on which the Mississippi is meandering includes low meander belt ridges and large flood-basin lowlands. Other surface features include abandoned sloughs, lakes, levees, bayous, and other small streams.

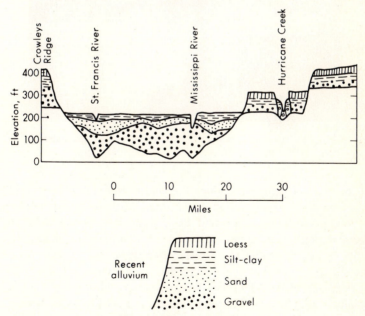

Fig. 6.4   A cross section of part of the alluvial plain of the Mississippi River. [From Fisk (1944).]

Floodplains of other rivers resemble that of the Mississippi but are not on so grand a scale.

Deltas

When a river flows into the sea or into any body of standing water such as a lake or pond, it drops its debris load, which is deposited as a delta. The form which such sediments take depends upon the character and quantity of the load and the waves and currents

Plate 15   Deposits made by a tributary entering a main stream. Near Yellow Springs, Ohio.

of the body of water into which the load is dumped. If the shoreline is exposed to strong waves or currents, if there is a strong tidal action, or if there is a small load, there will be no delta. If a delta is deposited, it may take any of a number of shapes (Fig. 6.5). It may resemble the Greek letter *delta* (Δ), as does that of the Nile; it may have the more common arcuate, or fan, shape, as does that of the Niger; or it may be composed of many branching channels which build out long fingers, such as the bird's foot delta of the Mississippi. Deltas may also be formed at the mouth of a drowned stream (estuary), with the load deposited in the narrow valley, as is happening in the Seine, Mackenzie, and Vistula Rivers.

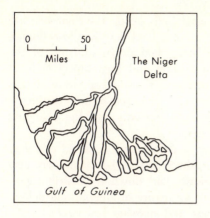

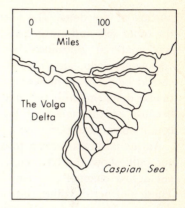

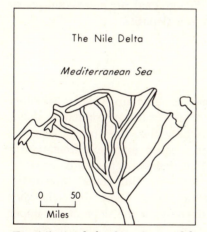

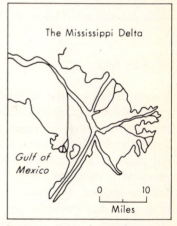

Fig. 6.5   Areal sketches of some deltas, indicating various shapes they may take.

The top surface of a delta is rather flat and forms a subaerial and subaqueous plain. It is covered with a set of almost flat-lying strata, composing the topset beds. These are usually fine-grained sands, silts, and clays and contain a great deal of organic matter. Immediately below these sediments are the foreset beds. They are coarser in texture and have a steeper dip. They make up the major portion of the delta. The bottomset beds lie on the floor beneath the other sets and are generally composed of very fine to colloidal-type material. Bottomset beds, being laid down in front of the advancing delta, are covered by foreset and then topset beds. It should be realized, however, that this is the ideal situation. A particular delta probably will not show all three sets of beds distinctly, because of the action of waves and currents and the changing conditions of transportation and load.

An actual cross section through a delta may be varied and may not only show the characteristic three sets of beds but may also cut across channel and bar deposits laid down by distributaries. These shifting distributaries cause a mixture of alluvial and deltaic deposits. Moreover, since lagoons and marshes are characteristic features of deltaic regions, the fine-grained organic sediments of these are also interbedded with deltaic deposits.

Alluvial fans

Either deltas or alluvial fans may be built up where a tributary enters a lower-gradient stream. Alluvial fans are similar to deltas but are deposited on land. Generally they are formed where a stream suddenly debouches from a steep mountain front onto a flat plain. It is commonly held that deposition occurs because the gradient is drastically reduced. However, Bull found that in the fans he studied, the gradient of the stream valley above the apex of the fan was the same, approximately, as the slope of the upper fan segment. Hence, deposition is the result of change in channel width and loss of volume as the stream flows out over the fan. Although decrease in depth causes increase in velocity, this is offset by volume reduction. The overall effect is a loss of transportive power.

These deposits are fan- or cone-shaped, with a marked apex at the point of emergence from the mountain front, and spreading radially outward onto the plain (Fig. 6.6) and merging with it. The steepest slope is at the apex, the ground slope becoming more and more gentle outward and downward. However, Yatsu pointed out that there is a definite slope discontinuity near the fan margin. In his analysis of fan sediments, he found that the break in fan

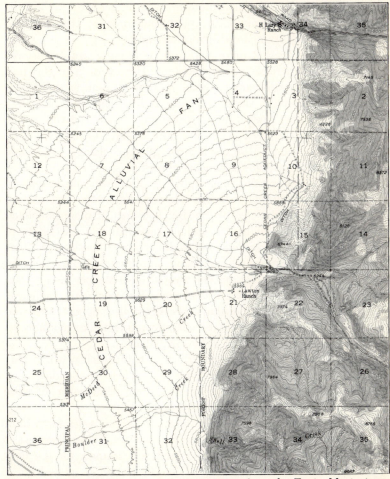

Fig. 6.6 Topographic map of an alluvial fan, from the Ennis, Mont., topographic quadrangle.

slope coincided with the boundary of gravel deposits. The debris composing a fan is generally gravel, with some sand, at the apex and grades out into finer material, sand and silt, at the margins. Ruling out tectonic causes, Yatsu related the break in slope to discontinuity in grain size of the fan materials.

Bull found that the surface slopes of some alluvial fans in California did not decrease at a uniform rate. Rather, he graphed the slopes as broken segments of straight-line profiles. He found no relation between grain-size distribution and fan slope, as did Yatsu, although he grants that there is a decrease in grain size downslope, as well as an increase in clay content. However, since the fans were in a tectonically active region, he thought that, as the stream channels successively steepened with uplift, their associated fan segments became steeper also. Although tectonic activity is the main cause of the breaks in these fan profiles, he thought such discontinuities could also result from climatic change or change of base level by eustatic movements of water.

Further, he related the geomorphology of alluvial fans to characteristics of their drainage basins. He found that the size of fans varied directly as the size of the drainage area of their associated streams. The slope of the fan surface varied directly as the steepness of the stream gradient and indirectly with basin size. Fans derived from regions with mudstone and shale lithology tended to be larger in area and thicker and to have steeper slopes than fans from drainage areas on sandstone. He concluded, therefore, that alluvial fan size and shape are controlled by the area and erodibility of their basins, by the climatic and tectonic environment, and by the adjacent fans and depositional basins.

Many alluvial fans are trenched, or cut, by washes which may contain water only during a flood. These tend to be deep and narrow and are generally formed during short-term climatic changes when rainfall is high and intense.

It often happens that a whole series of streams issues forth from a mountain front, each building up its own fan. When these grow until they meet, a coalescing alluvial fan is formed. Or the finer particles, washed down from the fan to its edges, may form a continuous plain. Such a plain, composed of finer material on the basinward edges of a number of fans, is called a *bahada*. Alluvial fans and bahadas are more easily seen in arid and semiarid regions and are thus considered to be characteristic landforms of these areas.

Thus, we see that the landforms created by river deposits depend on hydraulic characteristics of the stream and its channel, on the load it carries, and on the topographic characteristics of the land surface over which the stream flows. These, in turn, are dependent on the climate and geology of the region.

REFERENCES AND SELECTED READINGS

Blissenbach, E. (1954) Geology of alluvial fans in semi-arid regions: Geol. Soc. Am. Bull. 65, pp. 175–190.

Bull, W. B. (1963) Geomorphology of segmented alluvial fans in Western Fresno County, Calif.: U.S. Geol. Surv. Prof. Paper 352E.

——— (1964) Alluvial fans and near surface subsidence in Western Fresno County, Calif.: U.S. Geol. Surv. Prof. Paper 437A.

Colby, B. R. (1964) Scour and fill in sand-bed streams: U.S. Geol. Surv. Prof. Paper 462D.

Fisk, H. N. (1944) Geological investigation of the alluvial valley of the lower Mississippi River: Mississippi River Commission, Vicksburg, Miss.

Lattman, L. H. (1960) Cross section of a flood plain in a moist region of moderate relief: Jour. Sediment. Petrol., vol. 30, no. 2, pp. 275–282.

Leighley, J. B. (1934) Turbulence and the transportation of rock debris by streams: Geograph. Rev., vol. 24, pp. 453–464.

Leliavsky, S. (1955) An introduction to fluvial hydraulics: Constable, London.

Schumm, S. A., and R. W. Lichty (1963) Channel widening and flood plain construction along Cimarron River in southwestern Kans.: U.S. Geol. Surv. Prof. Paper 352D.

Sundborg, A. (1956) The river Klarälven, a study of fluvial processes; Geograph. Ann., vol. 38, pp. 127–316.

Wertz, J. B. (1963) Mechanism of erosion and deposition along channelways: Jour. Ariz. Acad. Sci., vol. 2, no. 4, pp. 146–163.

Wolman, M. G., and L. B. Leopold (1957) River flood plains: some observations on their formation: U.S. Geol. Surv. Prof. Paper 282C.

Yatsu, E. (1954) On the formation of slope discontinuity at fan margins: Inst. Nat. Resources (Japan) Misc. Rept., no. 36, pp. 57–64.

7

Slope and channel morphology

The longitudinal profile of a stream shows its slope, or gradient. It is the visual representation of the ratio of the fall of a stream to its length over a given reach, or a configuration of the channel bottom in longitudinal view. Most longitudinal profiles are concave upward (Fig. 7.1). Exceptions are certain ephemeral streams or rivers in arid or semiarid regions, where the volume of water decreases downstream, because of either seepage or evaporation. Deposition occurs when the volume of water cannot transport the load, giving a convex profile (Fig. 7.2). In the general case, the longitudinal profile may be smooth or broken, but it is concave upward.

Causes of concavity

Surrell believed that concavity of the profile was a result of three different regimes along

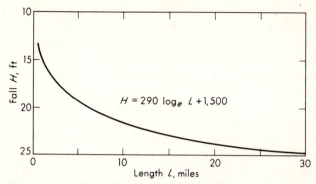

Fig. 7.1 Longitudinal profile of the Calfpasture River, Va., showing the usual concavity of stream profiles. [After Hack (1957).]

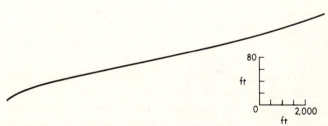

Fig. 7.2 Longitudinal profile of a stream in a semiarid region, showing a convex profile. [From Schumm (1961).]

the length of a stream. The upper reaches of a river he considered mainly areas of collection of water and erosion of the land surface; hence scour dominates toward the head of a stream. The lower reaches of a river are areas of deposition, with aggradation predominant. The middle area he regarded as one of transition between the two. The combination provides a concave profile along the stream length.

Others, Sternberg among them, thought that the determining factor in the concavity of a river profile was the downstream decrease in grain size of the load carried. Thus the gradient of a stream is steep at the head in order to maintain the velocity and competence to move the coarse debris which is supplied to it there. Downstream, the debris load of a river is much finer-grained, and the velocity required to carry it can be much lower. Therefore, the stream can flatten its gradient and still transport the load.

However, the concavity of the profile is probably the result, not of just one reason, but of a number of interdependent factors. It is the result of the balance of capacity and competence with the amount and caliber of the load and the effort of the river to maintain that balance throughout its length. If the capacity and competence are in excess of those required to transport the load, the river will lower its capacity and competence through modification of channel morphology and slope. Now, from Gilbert's experiments we have seen that a stream's ability to transport a given load depends upon the gradient of the stream, its volume, and the fineness of the particles comprising the load. Other observers have found that it also depends upon channel width and depth, bed roughness, and channel pattern. Theoretically, the river can alter any of these factors except volume and fineness of the load supplied. Here let us assume that it adjusts conditions to transport its load by modifying its gradient.

In general, discharge (except for ephemeral streams) increases downstream, and a rise in volume increases ability to transport. A stream with a larger discharge can maintain a given velocity with a lower slope. Moreover, discharge usually increases downstream at a faster rate than load. All these factors contribute to excess capacity and competence. Thus the stream can lower its gradient and still be able to carry its load. Observation has demonstrated that in most rivers the particle size of the load decreases downstream. Increase in fineness of the load increases ability to transport. Hence, again, the stream has excess ability for the grain size in transport, which enables it to lessen its slope. In addition, the cross-sectional area increases downstream, with resulting increase in capacity and competence. Therefore, again, slope can be reduced. Also, with greater depth and a finer load, relative roughness decreases downstream, resulting in less turbulence and thus less loss of energy. These factors combined mean that the river can maintain its ability to transport the load in a downstream direction and lower its slope. Hence, the profile is concave.

Adjustments in the profile

How does the stream make adjustments in its gradient in order to enable it to transport the load provided? If the river is unable to move its load below a given point on the profile, it will increase its gradient. It does this by depositing some of its load at the point of incompetency (Fig. 7.3*a*). This builds up the channel

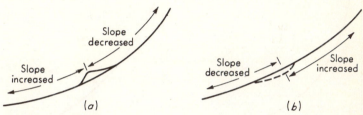

Fig. 7.3 Adjustments made by a river in its longitudinal profile. (*a*) Deposition to increase the gradient and (*b*) scour to decrease the gradient.

bed, causing an increased slope below the point and thus an increased ability to transport. This initial deposition at the same time results in a decreased gradient and a loss of transportive power above the given point. Hence the stream has to continue aggrading upstream, and there is a wave of aggradation up the channel.

If a stream has excess ability to transport and can carry more load than is supplied to it, it will lower its gradient. It does this by scouring its channel at the point of excess power (Fig. 7.3*b*). This gentles the slope below the given point but, at the same time, steepens the slope above the point. Hence a wave of erosion proceeds upstream.

Mathematical curves

Numerous attempts have been made to find a mathematical curve which best fits the longitudinal profile of rivers. Green proposed a logarithmic equation of the form

$$y = a - k \log (p - x) \qquad (7.1)$$

where y is elevation and x is distance along the stream, both measured from sea level. a, k, and p are constants, unique for each river. This equation is illustrated in general form in Fig. 7.4a. The

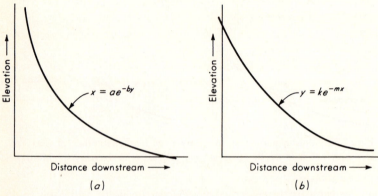

Fig. 7.4   Generalized graphs to represent equations of a stream profile.

curve is a straight line when plotted on a semilogarithmic scale, with vertical arithmetic and horizontal logarithmic scales. Streams with such a profile equation will be asymptotic to a line parallel to the vertical axis, never crossing the divide. However, the profile approaches and reaches sea level (the horizontal axis) as the stream erodes downward with time.

Another type of equation has been offered by Shulits in terms of distance along the stream and abrasion of the pebbles carried in the load,

$$s = s_0 e^{-ax} \qquad (7.2)$$

where s is slope of the channel bed, s_0 is the starting slope where the distance along the stream, x, is zero, and a is a coefficient of abrasion. In terms of elevation y and horizontal distance along the stream, x, this equation can be transformed into

$$y - y_0 = \frac{s_0}{a} (e^{ax} - 1) \tag{7.3}$$

This equation, shown graphically in Fig. 7.4b, shows that the stream will intersect and lower the divide with time. However, it is asymptotic to the horizontal axis and will never quite erode its bed to sea level, although it will approach it over a long period of time. Such a profile equation is a straight line on semilogarithmic paper, when elevation is plotted on the vertical logarithmic scale and distance on the horizontal arithmetic scale.

In deriving this equation, Shulits depended upon the statement of Sternberg that the size of particles in the bed material varies exponentially in a downstream direction so that

$$w = w_0 e^{-ax} \tag{7.4}$$

where w_0 is the original weight of a pebble, w is its weight at a given point downstream which is x distance from its origin, and a is the coefficient of wear. This decrease in grain size downstream has been confirmed by many field observations.

Other investigators have found that there is a definite relationship between stream gradient and stream length of the type

$$S = kL^n \tag{7.5}$$

where S is stream gradient at a given point, L is stream length from the head to that point, and k and n are empirical constants. From this relationship Hack derived two equations for the longitudinal profile,

$$H = k \ln L + C \qquad \text{when } n = -1 \tag{7.6}$$

$$H = \frac{k}{n+1} (L^{n+1} + C) \qquad \text{when } n \neq -1 \tag{7.7}$$

where H is fall, L is stream length, and n and k are constants as in Eq. (7.5) and C is a new constant. Putting together the facts that there is a relationship between slope and length and that particle size diminishes downstream, Hack arrived at an expression for the longitudinal profile as

$$H = \frac{25j^{0.6}}{0.6m} L^{0.6} + C \qquad (7.8)$$

where H, L, and C are as before and m and j are constants related to rate of change of particle size in moving downstream. If the size of grains on the bed remains constant, i.e., if $m = 0$, then the equation becomes

$$H = 25j^{0.6} \ln L + C \qquad (7.9)$$

Change of grain size downstream

The preceding analysis of stream gradient raises the question of the cause of diminution of particles downstream. This may result either from selective sorting or from abrasion. Are larger grains left behind and only finer ones transported because of loss of competency? Only if the stream were aggrading to steepen its slope would decrease in grain size downstream be a result of sorting, since coarser particles would be deposited first and the finer ones carried on. Or if the stream were losing volume downstream, as happens in arid regions or in areas of porous rock, this would bring about deposition of grains with sorting.

Then do the grains become smaller because of wear, as Sternberg surmised? Numerous laboratory studies have been made to determine rates of abrasion of particles in rotating barrels. These have shown that amount of abrasion depends upon the durability of the materials involved, the original size of the grains, and the size of associated particles in transport. In such experiments, quartz has been shown to be more resistant to abrasion than the feldspars or ferromagnesium minerals (hornblendes and pyroxenes) and graywacke more resistant than limestone. The size of grains also controls the rate of wear, gravels being reduced in size more quickly than sand. The size of associated particles is important, for in mixtures containing grains of various diameters the smaller grains erode away more quickly than larger ones. Studies in the field commonly indicate a much greater decrease in size than the rate of wear implied in laboratory experiments, although the rate of decrease varies greatly from stream to stream.

Factors such as parent material, weathering, and additions from tributaries may also influence the downstream change in grain size. Hack found that, in some streams he studied, particle size reflected the type of bedrock. Sandstone bedrock yielded larger load material, then shale, and limestone gave the finest. This is a result partly of resistance of the rock type to abrasion, partly of resistance to weathering, and partly of ease and method of breakage. Large boulders are often temporarily stored along a channel. Here they are exposed to weathering and to abrasion by material in transport, until they are broken and worn smaller and/or moved on.

If one assumes the reduction in particle size downstream to be a result of abrasion, the grain-size distribution should gradually change from coarse to fine in fluvial sediments from head to mouth. Yatsu, in investigations of river deposits, found this to be generally true. He also found that there was a relation between discontinuity of decrease in grain size downstream and discontinuity of slope. That is, as the grain size gradually diminished downstream, so did the river gradient. But an abrupt change from pebbles to sand in the bed of the stream was reflected in the longitudinal profile, which also showed an abrupt change in slope. He could not ascribe the break in profile to crustal movement or changes in sea level. Instead, he believed that the slope profile resulted from the discontinuity of grain-size distribution and thus reflected the balance (or lack of it) between tractive force and bed load.

Effects of lithology

Several investigators have inquired into the effect which rock type and lithology have on the longitudinal profile. Brush found in his studies of some streams in the Folded Appalachians of Pennsyl-

vania that there was a different relation of stream length to gradient
on the three different types of lithologies present.

On sandstone: $S = 0.046L^{-0.67}$ (7.10)

On shale: $S = 0.034L^{-0.81}$ (7.11)

On limestone: $S = 0.019L^{-0.71}$ (7.12)

where, in each case, S stands for stream gradient and L for length.
Gradient decreased downstream regardless of rock type, but its
rate of decrease varied significantly on the different rock units.
The average slope was found to be greater for any given length
on sandstone than on shale or limestone. In turn, stream gradients
on shale were steeper than those on limestone, for comparable
lengths.

Hack, in a study of rivers in Virginia and Maryland, also determined the relationship of slope to length on a variety of rock types
(Fig. 7.5). Sandstone, shale, and limestone are in the same order
as Brush found, except at longer distances, where limestone slopes
are greater than those on shale. One should keep several points
in mind in observing the results of these two studies. First, Brush
and Hack are comparing the gradients of stream lengths that are
equal and may thus be comparing a stretch without tributaries
with one having several. It has been pointed out previously that
tributaries affect the gradient of a main stream, since they add
volume and load. Second, streams in the Folded Appalachians
(whether in Virginia or Pennsylvania) are not flowing *on* the rock
units: they are flowing *across* them.

That the attitude, as well as the lithology, of the rock units
is important is shown by studies of Morisawa in the Appalachian
Plateau province. Here, streams flowing on flat-lying strata formed
steeper gradients on shale and limestone than on sandstone. It
seems, then, that when a stream flows *on* a resistant layer the
gradient is gentle and when it flows *through* or *across* a resistant
rock the gradient is steep. Morisawa found knicks in the river
profiles where sandstone layers were encountered. Gradients above
the knickpoint (on the sandstone) were gentle; gradients below
the knickpoint (through the sandstone) were steep.

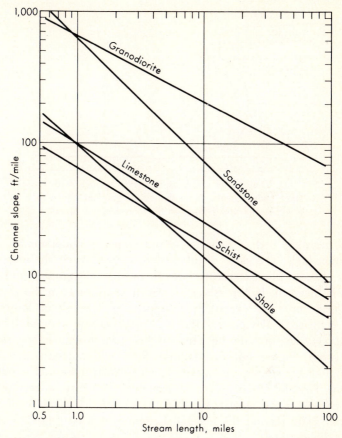

Fig. 7.5 Relation of stream length to gradient on different lithologies. [Redrawn from Hack (1957).]

Knickpoints

Since slope is actually determined by the corrasive power of the stream, bed resistance and structure, and the length of time that erosion has taken place, we may find falls and rapids in the longitudinal profile. Figure 7.6 gives an example of a stream flowing

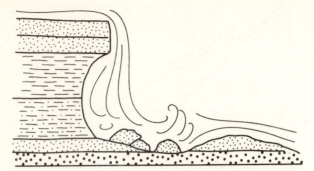

Fig. 7.6   Diagram of a falls on resistant cap rock, with less resistant beds beneath. Note flatness of gradient above the falls, where the stream flows *on* the more resistant layers.

on a resistant bed of flat-lying strata which is underlain by less resistant beds. The slope of the stream is very low on the resistant layer. Where the water cuts through the hard layer, the gradient is very steep; in fact, it is vertical. Such knickpoints in the profile are transitory and eventually disappear as a result of lowering and retreat. In the process the falls may become a rapid. These knickpoints are actually the cause of their own disappearance, since the steep slope results in shooting flow, with increased erosion from impact, eddies, and cavitation. Crickmay observed a cutoff in the Pembina River, Canada, which in 1947 had a knickpoint in bedrock at the breach. By 1956 the waterfall had retreated upstream 1,050 ft, and the channel bottom had been regraded over this whole stretch.

Studies of knickpoints in unconsolidated alluvium have been made in the laboratory by Brush and Wolman and in the field by Morisawa. Figure 7.7 shows the falls on Cabin Creek, Mont., as it was shortly after its formation in 1959. The knickpoint was formed in alluvium where a scarp, caused by an earthquake, crossed the stream. The point where the scarp originally crossed the stream was regraded and marked only by tremendously large boulders, which were too big to be moved.

Migration and destruction of these knickpoints depend upon the relation of competence to the size of material in the alluvium composing the falls. The finer material is removed first, large boulders being lowered in place or falling because of instability when the

Plate 16 Irregularities (knickpoints) in the slope of a stream, resulting from inequalities of lithologic resistance to erosion. Bouch's Falls, Panther Creek, N.Y. (Courtesy of G. Dougherty.)

smaller material is removed. Debris, washed down from the knickpoint, tends to be deposited below the falls, thus building up an oversteepened reach. In this way, the falls is reduced to a rapids and begins to lose its identity. The river thus decreases its slope over the stretch. It also reduces it by lengthening its course, meandering on the oversteepened reach. Rapids also form above the knickpoint by retreat of the original knick. Thus three things occur simultaneously: (1) lowering of the knickpoint in its original position by removal of material; (2) retreat of the top of the falls upstream; (3) deposition of material below the falls. All these events tend to obscure the knickpoint and restore a smooth profile.

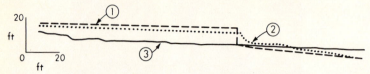

Fig. 7.7 Destruction of the knickpoint on Cabin Creek, Mont. The falls, formed by an earthquake, was in unconsolidated material which was washed away the following spring and the profile gradually regraded. (1) The profile immediately after formation of the falls. (2) An intermediate profile a few months later. (3) The regraded profile 3 years later.

The transverse profile

The transverse profile is the view of a section cut across the stream channel from bank to bank, perpendicular to the direction of flow. It shows the width, depth, and shape of the stream channel at any given point. One might say that every river has an infinite number of cross sections at any one given point. That is, the form of the cross section changes with any change of water surface with discharge.

Velocity and channel shape

The channel cross section is often expressed numerically as the form ratio, depth over width. A small form ratio represents a deep, narrow channel shape (Fig. 7.8). The Columbia River near the international boundary has a form ratio of 1/19 in the summer. At the same time of the year, the Platte River near Duncan, Nebr., has a form ratio of 1/160. The Columbia River can carry its load with a gradient of 2.2 ft/mile, whereas the Platte River requires a gradient of 5.6 ft/mile to transport its load. The Platte, with its heavy bed load and the volume of water supplied to it, finds that a wide, shallow cross section and steep gradient are necessary to carry the debris.

To explain this, we need to recall the Chézy equation,

$$V = C \sqrt{RS} \tag{3.8}$$

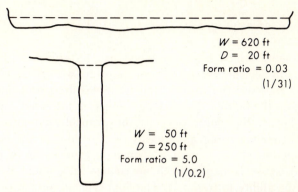

Fig. 7.8 Two channel cross sections to illustrate differences in form ratio.

In order to maintain a given velocity, then, if C remains constant, slope varies inversely as the hydraulic radius (depth). Let us also refer to Fig. 4.8, which shows the results of some flume experiments by Kennedy and Brooks. In these experiments a constant discharge of 0.50 cfs/ft and sand with a geometric mean grain size of 0.142 mm were used. These workers found that, for a constant discharge, depth depended on the rate of sediment transport. For a low rate of sediment discharge, the depth in the channel was great and velocity was low, while for a high rate of sediment transport, the depth of channel was small and velocity was high. Thus, for a constant stream discharge, an increase in sediment transport requires an increase in velocity and a corresponding decrease in depth.

The transporting efficiency of a channel form depends, in part, on the distribution of shear and velocity distribution, both of which vary with channel shape. We have seen (Fig. 3.3) that isovels of higher velocity lie closer to the sides in a narrow, deep channel and that the velocity gradient is highest close to the walls. This means that in such a channel form there will be a higher rate of shear near the banks than on the bed. On the other hand, a wide, shallow channel has a higher velocity gradient and a greater rate of shear near the bed than near the channel sides, which aids entrainment and transport.

Influence of sediment type

The ease with which banks and bed can be eroded will allow the stream to develop a channel form consistent with the erodibility of the material and the velocity and shear distributions. Scour taking place on the bottom of a channel results in decreased capacity, since it lowers the slope, deepens the channel, and lowers the velocity. Scour occurring more easily on the sides of the channel will widen the channel, with a change in form so as to give a relative decrease in depth. With no change in gradient this will increase the ability to transport. The final channel form will reflect the balance of bank and bed resistance to side and bottom velocity and shear. The mutual adjustment of the cross section with the gradient provides the capacity and competence needed to transport the load.

In some flume studies, Wolman and Brush found that the size of sand comprising the bank material determined the shape of channels in alluvial material. In fine, cohesive sand, width and depth of the channel varied as a power function of discharge. In coarser, less cohesive sand, the channel size and form also depended upon discharge but varied almost directly as a linear function of discharge. In the coarser sand, the angle of repose was important in determining the shape of the channel.

In investigations on larger rivers of the Great Plains, Schumm confirmed that the type of sediment in the beds and banks exerted a control on the cross-sectional form. Where the alluvium was sandy or composed of gravel with a low content of silt and clay, stream channels were wide and shallow, with a relatively steep gradient. Figure 7.9 shows the relationship between width and depth of channel for certain individual rivers. Each point on the graph represents a cross section where the weighted mean percent of silt-clay is about the same. Schumm thinks that the position of the regression line depends on the amount of silt-clay in the channel. Sand Creek, farthest to the left, has a weighted mean percent silt-clay of 21.7 and the Smoky Hill–Kansas River, farthest to the right, has a silt-clay content of 3.4. However, mean annual discharge is also important in shaping the channel, and Schumm considers the shift of the Smoky Hill and Powder Rivers regression

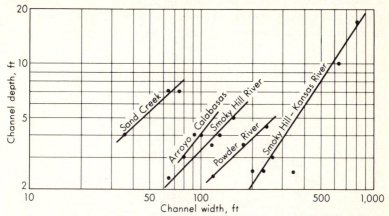

Fig. 7.9 Relation of channel width to channel depth in alluvial streams on the Great Plains. [After Schumm (1960).]

lines to the right to be a result of larger discharge. He also found that in a downstream direction along the Smoky Hill River, as the silt-clay content decreased, there was a large increase in channel width, relative to depth. And whenever there was a local increase in silt-clay in the channel, depth increased greatly relative to width.

Schumm related width-depth ratio to the percent silt-clay in the channel and found that the amount of extremely fine material seems to characterize the resistance of the channel to erosion. Material with a large amount of silt-clay is cohesive and tends to resist erosion. Hence a channel in this type of alluvium will be narrower, since it can withstand higher shear. On the other hand, there is little or no cohesion in material of coarse sand. Sands are thus easily eroded, and the loose grains are removed immediately. They tend to have a wide, shallow cross section.

Changes in cross section

Variations in channel cross sections of certain streams were investigated by Leopold and Maddock and by Leopold and Miller. As one would expect, when discharge changes at a given point along a stream channel, there is a corresponding change in the width, depth, and velocity of flow. The relationship of each of these factors to discharge is a straight line (Fig. 7.10a) and can be expressed

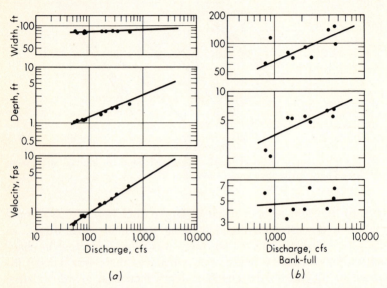

Fig. 7.10 Relationship of variations in discharge to width, depth, and velocity: (a) at a station on the Brandywine Creek at Embreeville, Pa; (b) in a downstream direction along the Brandywine Creek. [Both from Wolman (1955).]

as a series of empirical equations,

$$W = aQ^b \tag{7.13}$$

$$D = cQ^f \tag{7.14}$$

$$V = kQ^m \tag{7.15}$$

where W is width of the water surface, D is its depth, V is velocity of flow, Q is discharge, and a, b, c, f, k, and m are empirical constants. But since discharge equals cross-sectional area times velocity [Eq. (2.2)] and

$$WDV = ackQ^{b+f+m}$$

then

$$ack = 1 \quad \text{and} \quad b + f + m = 1$$

Wolman gives the following equations for Brandywine Creek at Cornog, Pa.:

$$W = 37Q^{0.04}$$

$$D = 17Q^{0.40}$$

$$V = 16Q^{0.52}$$

Whether the exponent for width or depth is larger probably depends on the load and the composition of bed and bank material. However, not enough data have been gathered to determine the exact effect of these variables on the value of the exponents.

Proceeding downstream on the same river, width, depth, and velocity all increase regularly with discharge (Fig. 7.10*b*). So another, similar set of equations can represent these changes,

$$W = hQ^r \tag{7.16}$$

$$D = pQ^s \tag{7.17}$$

$$V = nQ^t \tag{7.18}$$

In general, width seems to change more rapidly than depth in a downstream direction. It is interesting that sometimes velocity decreases downstream. Perhaps this means that the load of such a stream becomes significantly finer or less in proportion to the amount of discharge gained.

Changes during flood discharge

It has been demonstrated that width and depth are adjusted by a river for any discharge at a given point, as well as in a downstream direction. Let us examine in more detail the changes that occur in channel shape during extremely large discharges. An example of a flood on the San Juan River is presented by Leopold and Maddock. During the rising stages of the flood, as the water surface rose, the level of the channel bottom also rose. Along with these changes, the width of the water surface increased only slightly, while depth, velocity, and amount of suspended load increased greatly (Fig. 7.11). These cross-sectional changes of this particular river are probably a result of the composition of bed and bank material in relation to load. At about 5,000 to 6,000 cfs, there was a lessening in the rate of increase of suspended-sediment load, as well as a lessening of the rate of velocity increase. At the same time, the elevation of the water surface and channel depth increased more rapidly. During the latter part of the rising stage, scour of the channel took place, and the stream bed was lowered.

During the recession of the floodwaters, decrease of width, depth, velocity, and suspended-load concentration was regular. Channel elevation remained almost the same: neither erosion nor deposition took place. Note that, while width follows approximately the same curve on rising and falling stages, there are two depths and two velocities corresponding to an increase or decrease in the suspended load. Analysis of these changes shows that load, as well as discharge itself, seems to be important in the adjustments which a stream makes in its morphology.

Colby has interpreted channel adjustments to increased discharge in a way different from that of Leopold and Maddock. He believes that depth adjustments in a channel cross section are changes, not in elevation of the stream bed itself, but merely in the water surface. Hence, the average elevation of the bottom of a river bed is stable during a flood. This is because of the principle of continuity of sediment discharge, which states that the movement of sediment into and out of a reach is balanced by the gain or loss of sediment in the reach. And since as much sediment is carried out of the reach by flood waters as is carried in, the bed elevation remains stable.

In any event, these investigations have shown that width and depth tend to vary regularly with increasing or decreasing discharge. If discharge is held constant and width decreases, then

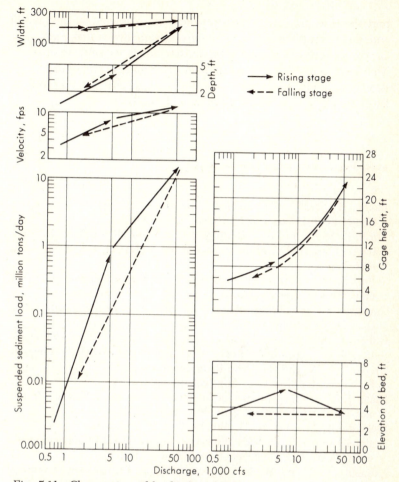

Fig. 7.11 Changes in width, depth, velocity, gage height, bed elevation, and suspended sediment load during a flood on the San Juan River. [From Leopold and Maddock (1955).]

the channel should be deepened by scour. This is because of the increase in velocity and transportive power which accompanies narrowing of the channel.

Thus, we see that the hydrodynamics of a river call for a configuration of longitudinal and transverse profiles which best transport the discharge and load supplied to it. The comparative width and depth and the gradient of any stream depend in large part on the material through which the stream is carving its channel. The long-term controls of channel morphology are climate and geology, because these determine the load, discharge, and erodibility of the channel and thus the channel form itself.

REFERENCES AND SELECTED READINGS

Baulig, H. (1926) La notion de profil d'equilibre, histoire et critique: Congr. Intern. Geograph., 1925, vol. 3, pp. 51–63.

Brush, L. M., Jr. (1961) Drainage basins, channels and flow characteristics of selected streams in central Pennsylvania: U.S. Geol. Surv. Prof. Paper 282F.

Colby, B. R. (1961) Effect of depth of flow on discharge of bed material: U.S. Geol. Surv. Water Supply Paper 1498D.

Crickmay, C. H. (1960) Lateral activity in a river of northwestern Canada: Jour. Geol., vol. 48, no. 4, pp. 377–391.

Gilbert, G. K. (1877) Report on the geology of the Henry Mountains: U.S. Geol. Geog. Surv. Rocky Mountain Region, GPO, Washington.

Green, J. F. N. (1934) The River Mole: its physiography and superficial deposits: Proc. Geol. Soc., vol. 45, pp. 35–59.

Hack, J. T. (1957) Studies of longitudinal stream profiles in Virginia and Maryland: U.S. Geol. Surv. Prof. Paper 294B.

Kennedy, J. F., and N. H. Brooks (1963) Laboratory study of an alluvial stream at constant discharge: Proc. Federal Interagency Sediment. Conf., U.S. Dept. Agr. ARS 970, pp. 320–329.

Leopold, L. B., and W. B. Langbein (1962) The concept of entropy in landscape evolution: U.S. Geol. Surv. Prof. Paper 500A.

——— and T. Maddock (1955) The hydraulic geometry of stream channels and some physiographic implications: U.S. Geol. Surv. Prof. Paper 252.

Morisawa, M. (1962) Quantitative geomorphology of some watersheds in the Appalachian Plateau: Geol. Soc. Amer. Bull., vol. 73, pp. 1025–1046.

Schumm, S. A. (1960) The shape of alluvial channels in relation to sediment type: U.S. Geol. Surv. Prof. Paper 352B.

——— (1961) Effect of sediment characteristics on erosion and deposition in ephemeral stream channels: U.S. Geol. Surv. Prof. Paper 352C.

Shulits, S. (1941)   Rational equation of river bed profiles: Trans. Am. Geophys. Union, vol. 41, pp. 622–629.

Surrell, A. (1870)   Etude sur les torrents des Hautes-Alpes: L'Academie des Sciences, Paris.

Wolman, M. G. (1955)   The natural channel of Brandywine Creek, Pennsylvania: U.S. Geol. Surv. Prof. Paper 271.

Woodford, A. O. (1951)   Stream gradients and the Monterey Sea valley: Geol. Soc. Am. Bull. 62, pp. 799–852.

Yatsu, E. (1954)   On the formation of slope discontinuity at fan margins: Inst. Nat. Resources (Japan) Misc. Rept., no. 36, pp. 57–64.

8

The graded profile or the steady state

We have seen how the adjustment of a stream to the many and varied conditions of flow is reflected in its morphology, i.e., in its longitudinal and cross-sectional profiles. Emphasis has generally been placed on the adjustment of the gradient, and a stream was said to be ungraded if it had an uneven longitudinal profile, with ponds, falls, rapids, and shoals (Fig. 8.1). In such a stream, wherever there is a velocity increase, erosion will occur to lessen the gradient, and where there is a velocity decrease, aggradation will occur to steepen the slope. The stream thus tends toward elimination of irregularities and the establishment of a smoothly concave profile (Fig. 8.2). This smooth profile has been taken to mean that an equilibrium has been attained so that the stream has just that slope which provides the competency and capacity to transport its load. The stream is now said to be *graded.*

The equilibrium profile

The idea of an equilibrium profile was reached early in the seventeenth century, when Guglielmi concluded that a river will modify its channel, either eroding or depositing, until an equilibrium has

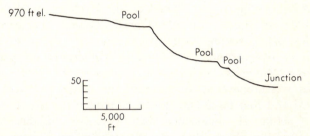

Fig. 8.1 Longitudinal profile of a stretch of Yellow Springs Creek, Ohio, showing many pools and a generally uneven profile.

been reached between energy and resistance. He stated that such equilibrium profiles are concave and their slopes vary with velocity of flow, load, and size of bed material. The terms *pente d'equilibre* and *régime* were commonly used in France to describe this condition of balance in a river. Hettner expressed the profile of equilibrium as a slope which is determined by a relationship in which discharge and velocity balance the mass and caliber of the load.

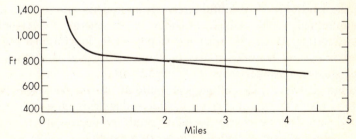

Fig. 8.2 Longitudinal profile of Bays Branch, Davis Creek, W.Va., showing a smooth, concave slope.

However, he realized that a true mathematical balance does not occur and suggested that the real stream profile will be steeper than the profile of equilibrium, in which case erosion takes place, or not so steep as the profile of equilibrium, in which case deposition takes place. He also stated that the actual profile which is established by the stream is a function of high-water or flood discharge.

American geologists contributed to the development of the idea of a profile of equilibrium with Powell's concept of a base level toward which a stream lowers its bed and by the many fundamentals of river erosion elucidated by Gilbert. In his paper on the Henry Mountains, Gilbert noted that the ability of a stream to erode was proportional to the resistance of the rock over which it flowed and that force and resistance tended toward an equilibrium of action. He understood that rivers are self-adjusting and emphasized the effects that changes on one reach have on the channel both upstream and down. Thus the whole system was interdependent. He thought that changes in declivity (slope) were most important and stated that a stream could not remain in equilibrium unless the energy lost by erosion and transportation was made up by an increase in energy from an increased gradient.

The concept of grade

Gilbert was the first to use the term *graded stream*, but Davis defined and elaborated upon the theme. Davis enlarged the concept, working it to fit into his theory of the cyclic development of the landscape. A youthful stream is ungraded, with an irregular longitudinal profile which provides much energy for vigorous downcutting. When the river has smoothed its longitudinal profile and is cutting laterally, it has become mature and is graded. In this stage it meanders over its floodplain and has reached an equilibrium between side-cutting and building up its floodplain. Old age is reached when the river meanders sluggishly on a very wide floodplain, lacking energy to either erode or deposit material. At this point the river is graded from head to mouth.

Davis stated that grade was a condition of balance between

corrasion and deposition, between degradation and aggradation. It is brought about by the ability of a river to adjust its capacity to work in response to changes in the amount of work to be done. When these two factors are equal, the stream is graded. Once a river does reach grade, it strives to maintain it. Hence, any change in the work to be done will result in a change in ability to reach a new balance. Davis envisaged the adjustments made by the stream in reaching and maintaining grade to be adjustments in slope. However, he emphasized the fact that attainment of grade did not mean that the slope of a stream would be now and forever after the same.

It is too often implied . . . that when a river is once balanced between erosion and deposition its slope thenceforward remains constant. . . . Such is evidently not the case. . . . The balanced condition of any stream can be maintained only by an equally continuous, though small, change of river slope.[1]

Grade thus implies both stability and gradual change. Davis also saw that, not only would the profile change with time, but it would also vary at different points along the stream. He pointed out that different streams, flowing under different environmental conditions, would result in different curves for the graded slope profile. He concluded, therefore, that there was no one graded profile, even for a single stream; hence it would be extremely difficult to generalize and obtain the one profile of equilibrium for all graded rivers.

Kesseli defined a graded river as one where there is a balance of energy and load. Mackin defined the concept of grade as a long-term balance between erosion and deposition.

A graded stream is one in which, over a period of years, slope is delicately adjusted to provide, with available discharge and with prevailing channel characteristics, just the velocity required for the transportation of the load provided. . . . The graded stream is a system in equilib-

[1] W. M. Davis, Geographical essays: Ginn, Boston, 1909 (republished 1954, Dover, New York), p. 398.

rium . . . any change in any of the controlling factors will cause a displacement in a direction that will tend to absorb the effect of change.[2]

Again, the main characteristic by which a stream adjusts and maintains the balanced or graded condition is the slope. Mackin did, however, acknowledge that adjustment could be made, and equilibrium achieved again, by changes in other channel characteristics such as depth or width.

Stream regimen

Some American geologists, following the terminology common in Europe, used the term *in regimen* (or *in regime*) to apply to a stream which had reached equilibrium between erosion and deposition. This term has not become popular among American geomorphologists, although it is used by engineers. Hydraulic engineers say that a stream is in regime when it can adjust its longitudinal slope and cross-sectional form so as to maintain a channel that is stable, i.e., a channel in which neither scour nor deposition takes place. The term is not a good one, as regimen is also used to denote the total economy or habit of a stream.

Dynamic equilibrium

Some geologists have questioned whether or not a stream ever attains a real equilibrium between load and ability to transport. Gilbert himself mentions that this condition is so hard to maintain that rivers are always either eroding or depositing. Instead, it has been suggested by Wolman and others that a river reaches a quasi equilibrium or dynamic equilibrium which is a fluctuating or changing balance. Also, since part of the river may be in balance while other stretches are not, the whole profile itself is not in equilibrium.

[2] J. H. Mackin, The concept of the graded river: Geol. Soc. Am. Bull., vol. 59, p. 471, 1948.

This seems to be a matter of semantics. It has been pointed out that Davis realized that the equilibrium was not exact; it was not a mathematical balance. Mackin defended this type of equilibrium with an emphasis on the long-term period of time. A river may scour its channel during a flood or aggrade it during a period of low flow, but, looked at over a period of time long enough to include all the transient fluctuations of discharge and load, a graded stream will show an equilibrium of action resulting in a stable channel. If equilibrium is used in this broad sense, the term *quasi* or *dynamic equilibrium* is superfluous.

The steady state

The concept of a steady state in an open system has been applied to streams by Strahler, Culling, and others. Because matter and energy enter and leave the system, we can consider an individual stream, as well as a whole drainage basin, an open system. Such open systems are characterized by the exchange of material and energy with, and continuous interaction on, the surroundings, in this case channel, ground surface, and even the air above. In open systems the rates of import and export of material and energy will become balanced so that an equilibrium is reached, called the *steady state*. In this stage, the system is self-regulatory; any change in the contributing environment results in a compensating change in the system.

If we consider a stream over a long period of time, the fluctuations in load and flow will be minimal and the discharge and load can be considered constant. When the rates of import and export of material are equal, i.e., when the channel is stable and is neither eroded nor silted up, the stream has reached a steady state. Any change which upsets the balance will be compensated for by a suitable adjustment in gradient or channel form. The term steady state, then, can be applied to rivers which have reached a stable condition of self-regulation. Stream-channel characteristics are constantly being altered to account for changes in the environment, and over a long period of time there is an equilibrium flow of water and debris in and out of the system. Although the steady state itself is time-independent and the flow of matter and energy through the system has reached a balance, the morphology of the river and its drainage basin is not static. Material is constantly being removed from the watershed, and there are changes in the surface and fluvial landforms.

Since the term equilibrium is so intimately connected with slope in geomorphic thought, and since it has now been determined that a stream adjusts many of its characteristics other than slope in response to environment, we should substitute steady state for equilibrium in the definition of grade. Moreover, this would prevent any disagreement over the use of equilibrium, quasi equilibrium, or dynamic equilibrium. A graded stream, therefore, is one in which a steady state has been reached such that, over a period of time, the discharge and load entering the system are balanced by the discharge and load leaving the system. The steady state is achieved and maintained by mutual interaction of channel characteristics such as gradient, cross-sectional form, roughness, and channel pattern. It is a self-regulatory system; any change in the controlling factors will cause a displacement in a direction that will tend to absorb the effect of the change.

Criteria for grade

Now, how can we determine whether or not a stream has reached a steady state? We can no longer use the smoothly concave longitudinal profile as an indication, because it has been shown that streams with irregular profiles are at grade. Wolman, for example, determined that Brandywine Creek has achieved grade; yet its profile is very irregular (Fig. 8.3). So although a stream's slope may be uneven, it may still have a stable channel. Despite the irregularities of the profile, any particle that is removed from the channel bed is replaced by another. Thus, one criterion for grade would be stability of the channel, or the tendency of the channel to regain the same form after a cycle of hydraulic regimen. If a bar is swept away with rising water, it will be reestablished at low water; if a channel is filled, it will be scoured out again. Wertz found that the scour and fill which occurred in the rivers

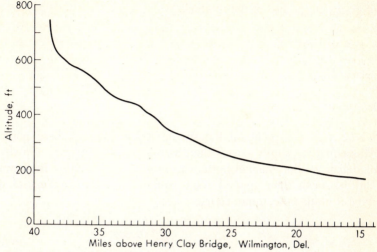

Fig. 8.3 Longitudinal profile of Brandywine Creek. [After Wolman (1955).]

he studied were simply a redistribution of alluvium in the channel floor.

Lokhtine tried to establish a stability criterion, or coefficient of fixation, to determine whether river channels were stable or not. He concluded that, if the ratio of average grain size to channel slope were low for a given stream, the channel would be unstable. If the grain size–slope ratio were high, the channel would be stable. This ratio for the Vistula River is 3.1 cm, and that of the Po River is 3.3 cm. Both these rivers have beds which are mobile. The grain size–slope ratio for the Dneister and Danube Rivers is 166 cm. The channels of both are considered stable.

Ichikawa and Ishikawa also used the criterion of grain size on the channel bed to determine whether or not the Doki River in Japan was graded. They decided that, if the stream were at grade, there should be an equilibrium between the frictional resistance of the bed alluvium and the tractive force exerted on it. Since bed material decreases in size downstream, tractive force and bed resistivity also decrease. If λd_m represents the resistivity of the bed, where $\lambda = 100\% - \%d_m$ and d_m is the mean diameter of grains on the bed of the channel,

$$x = a + b \log \lambda d_m \qquad (8.1)$$

or

$$\lambda d_m = 10^{x+a/b} \qquad (8.2)$$

where x is any point on the stream, taken above a base point. This equation simply means that, as one moves upstream, the size of debris on the channel bottom increases exponentially. Ichikawa and Ishikawa then applied Aki's equation for the gradient of a river at grade in its upper course,

$$i = I_0 \times 10^{\frac{5}{3.5}(x-x_0)/b} + \frac{3.45}{3.5b} H_0 \times 10^{\frac{1.5}{3.5}(x_0-x)/b} \qquad (8.3)$$

where i is the theoretical graded slope at x distance from a base point x_0, I_0 is the gradient of the river bed at the base point, and H_0 is the depth of water at that point. b is the empirical constant in Eq. (8.1). These workers found that the actual gradient of the Doki River is much steeper than the theoretical graded one would be. In actuality, also, the river is aggrading its channel and so may be considered unstable.

Because of the fact that rock resistance should play no part in determining erosion in a graded stream, another indication of grade would be lack of scour in soft material. Mackin emphatically says that the graded profile is a slope of transportation and, as such, is not influenced by rock resistance. He points out, in discussing the steep gradient of the Clark Fork, Mont., in which gravels were carried over a channel composed of till, lake clays, silts, gravels, and bedrock, that the high slopes were maintained of necessity. He says that, in order to transport the amount and size of the load given the river, a steep gradient would have been maintained even in cream cheese. Indeed, one of his criteria for a graded river is that the profile cuts smoothly across rocks of varying resistance without a break.

But rock resistance certainly must have an effect upon the slope during the process of establishing the stream morphology which becomes stable with the attainment of grade. And it is certain that the erodibility of the bed and banks helps determine the manner of adjustment to changes in load and discharge after grade has been achieved. Investigators who have inquired into the effect which lithology has on the longitudinal profile find that there is a different slope for graded streams flowing on different rock types. Perhaps this is why Brandywine Creek and others offer a broken profile, though graded. Since equilibrium profiles differ on different rock types, a composite profile of a stream flowing over various lithologies will show breaks where the stream flows from one type of rock to another. Yet each stretch may be graded.

An examination of terrace remnants may supply evidence that a stream is graded. The similarity of longitudinal profiles of the terrace and the present stream will show that the river has maintained the same gradient over a long period of time and is therefore graded. However, Culling pointed out that, if renewal of downcutting occurred over and over again after only short periods of stillstand and before readjustment is complete, the terrace surfaces will not be parallel to each other or to the present stream. Machida also found this to be the case in the terraces along the Kuji and Ara Rivers in Japan. Because of recurring tectonic movements at close time intervals which deformed the terraces, their surfaces were not parallel to the present-day river floor or to each other.

The important basic criterion for determining whether or not a stream is at grade is stability of the channel over a long period of time. If the same amount of material leaves the system as enters it, and if the overall channel characteristics provide the ability to transport all the load and convey it out of the system, the stream has reached a steady state and is graded.

The stable channel

A stream in the steady state, then, has a stable channel, i.e., a channel in which neither erosion nor deposition takes place. The shape of such a channel is dependent upon a number of factors. These are slope, roughness, velocity, velocity distribution, boundary shear, and discharge. It depends upon the mutual adjustment of width and depth and the side slopes of the channel. The material transported is important, as well as how it is transported—as bed or suspended load. It depends, also, upon the straightness or sinuosity of the channel and the uniformity of flow. And finally it depends upon the resistance of the banks and bed to erosion.

Engineers have, of course, been greatly concerned with the shape of nonerodible and nonsilting channels. In the course of their investigations, a number of empirical relationships have been established. Kennedy developed formulas defining the critical velocity which can be attained in a channel which is stable. The general formula was

$$V_c = aD^m \tag{8.4}$$

where V_c is velocity at which neither erosion nor deposition occurs, D is depth, and a and m are empirically determined. As D reaches a limiting value, the river banks will be eroded. Both a and m vary with differing channel widths.

Lacey, in discussing silt-stable channels, related the constant a to the physical morphology of the channel and the size of silt carried in transport. He also formulated an equation for silt-stable discharge in an alluvial channel as

$$Qf^2 = 3.8V_0^6 \tag{8.5}$$

where Q is silt-stable discharge, V_0 is the critical velocity at which neither erosion nor deposition occurs in the channel, f is a silt factor determined by

$$f = \frac{a}{1.17} \tag{8.6}$$

and a is the constant in Eq. (8.4).

Schumm suggests that the correlation of width-depth ratio of channel cross section and size of grain in the channel bed can be used as a criterion for a silt-stable channel. He found that stable channels fell on or close to the regression line

$$F = 255M^{-1.08} \tag{8.7}$$

where *F* is width-depth ratio and *M* is weighted mean percent silt-clay (Fig. 8.4). He considers that cross sections which fall above the line are aggrading channels, whereas those below the line are degrading.

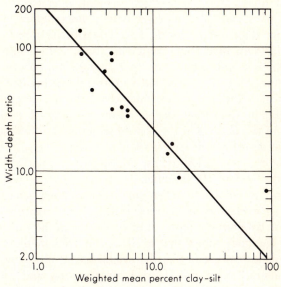

Fig. 8.4 Width-depth ratio as related to silt-clay content of channel material. [After Schumm (1960).]

Adjustments in the graded stream

Graded streams are self-regulatory and are able to adjust their characteristics to compensate for any change in the environment. These outside effects may include an alteration in volume of flow brought on by change of climate, vegetative cover, or any other factor instrumental in changing the amount of water supplied to the stream. Or the environmental change may be in the amount or caliber of the load. The river will adjust to the new conditions by changing its slope, its cross section, the roughness of its bed, its length, or the pattern of its channel. It may change any one or a combination of these characteristics, whichever it can, in order to maintain the balance between its ability to transport and the load provided.

In particular, if a stream has to increase its competence or capacity, it may do so by steepening its gradient. If conditions change so that a river can carry its load with a lower gradient, it will decrease its slope—as rivers do in a downstream direction. In a study of changes in channel gradients above gully control structures, Woolhiser and Lenz found that aggradation occurred above the structures. Deposition continued upstream but became progressively less until the new profile intersected the old, original slope. The new equilibrium slope depended on the original gradient, on the width of the channel at the control structure, and on the height of the inlet above the deepest part of the original channel. Below such structures and below dams, adjustment is usually made by scour of the bed of the channel. However, channel degradation below dams is not to be taken for granted. Such scouring may be inhibited by factors of bedrock controls, load contributions by downstream tributaries, or growth of vegetation in the channel. Leopold and Maddock found that a change of load in the Colorado River below a dam resulted in the establishment of a new equilibrium by alterations of the channel cross section and roughness, not by a change of slope. The decrease in load was compensated for by a decrease in channel width and an increased depth, while gradient remained fairly constant. Thus the stream lowered its velocity, not by scour, but by changing its form ratio. At the same time, the river increased the roughness of the channel bottom. Apparently, increase in bed roughness aided in reducing capacity and competence.

Brice found that increased discharge at tributary junctions on the Loup River in Nebraska did not result in a slope change. The gradient at junctions remained the same, but the channel cross section was altered to accommodate the increased discharge. Colby believes, however, that most depth adjustments are not really adjustments in the channel bed and walls but are simply cross-sectional changes brought about by adjustment of the water surface only.

Rubey has summed up the situation in what may be called an

equation of grade,

$$SF = \frac{kL^aD^b}{Q^c} \tag{8.8}$$

where S is the graded slope, F is the form ratio which has the greatest capacity for tractive load, L is the amount of load, D is average diameter of the bed load, and Q is discharge. Any change in the members of the right side of the equation will cause a compensating change in either or both of the factors on the left side. We can revise this equation to read

$$nSF = \frac{kL^aD^b}{Q^c} \tag{8.9}$$

where n is channel roughness. A stream which has reached the steady state, then, and is graded will strive to maintain its capacity and competence so that they are just equal to those required to transport the load provided, with available discharge. It does this by mutual adjustments in the longitudinal profile, cross-sectional morphology, and channel roughness.

REFERENCES AND SELECTED READINGS

Brice, J. C. (1964)   Channel patterns and terraces of the Loup River in Nebraska: U.S. Geol. Surv. Prof. Paper 422D.

Chorley, R. J. (1962)   Geomorphology and general systems theory: U.S. Geol. Surv. Prof. Paper 500B.

Culling, W. E. H. (1957)   Multicyclic streams and the equilibrium theory of grade: Jour. Geol., vol. 65, pp. 259–274.

Ichikawa, M., and Y. Ishikawa (1965)   Fluvial deposits and the grade of the river floor of the Doki, Japan: Tokyo Kyoiku Daigaku Sci. Rept., no. 83.

Inglis, C. (1948)   Historical note on empirical equations developed by engineers in India for flow of water and sand in alluvial channels: Intern. Hydraulic Res., Second Meeting, Stockholm 7–9, VI, app. 5, pp. 1–14.

Kennedy, R. G. (1895)   Prevention of silting in irrigation canals: Proc. Inst. Civil Engrs., part 1, p. 281.

Kesseli, J. E. (1941)   Concept of the graded river: Jour. Geol., vol. 49, pp. 561–588.

Lacey, G. (1930)   Stable channels in alluvium: Proc. Inst. Civil Engrs., vol. 229, pp. 259–384.

Machida, T. (1960)   Fluvial terraces along the River Kuji and the River Ara, Kanto District, Japan: Tokyo Kyoiku Daigaku Sci. Rept., no. 64.

Mackin, J. H. (1948)   Concept of the graded river: Geol. Soc. Am. Bull., vol. 59, pp. 463–512.

Rubey, W. W. (1933)   Equilibrium conditions in debris-laden streams: Trans. Am. Geophys. Union, vol. 14, pp. 497–505.

———— (1952)   Geology and mineral resources of the Hardin and Brussels quadrangles, Illinois, U.S. Geol. Surv. Prof. Paper 218.

Schumm, S. A. (1960)   The shape of alluvial channels in relation to sediment type: U.S. Geol. Surv. Prof. Paper 352B.

Strahler, A. N. (1952)   Dynamic basis of geomorphology: Geol. Soc. Am. Bull., vol. 63, pp. 923–938.

Wolman, M. G. (1955)   The natural channel of Brandywine Creek, Pennsylvania: U.S. Geol. Surv. Prof. Paper 271.

Woolhiser, D. A., and A. T. Lenz (1965)   Channel gradients above gully-control structures: Proc. Am. Soc. Civil Engrs., Jour. Hydraulics Div., vol. 91, pp. 165–187.

9

The channel pattern

Looked at from above or on a map, a stream may present a course which is straight, meandering, or braided. Some rivers have a well-developed sinuosity, whereas others are just slightly winding. A meandering stream may flow with the winding channel confined by and touching the valley walls, or it may have a channel with very contorted bends sprawled on a floodplain. Braiding is the division of a single channel into two or more anastomosing channelways. Many rivers exhibit each of these three channel patterns (straight, meandering, or braided) somewhere along their lengths. Investigations show that, not only are cross-sectional morphology and longitudinal profile of a river adjusted to environmental controls of load and discharge, but so also is the map plan of the channel.

Straight channels

If we take the deepest points on a stream channel and join them with a line, we have marked what is called the *thalweg* of the channel. Now, although the stream may have straight banks, the thalweg winds its way from side to side within the water. Moreover, the profile of a straight stretch shows a series of pools and riffles which is very much like the profile of a meandering or braided stream.

Plate 17 Sinuous channel of the Genesee River, N.Y., incised into sediments of the Appalachian Plateau. These are probably original first-cycle meanders.

Let us consider again the nature of flow of water in natural channels. There is a primary forward, or downstream, turbulent flow with mixing of various fluid masses. In addition, there is a secondary flow of surface water moving in toward the center of the stream and downward, and a movement of bottom water outward toward the walls and up. This combination of forward and sideward flow produces a spiral, or helical, movement of the whole water mass. Also, irregularities of the channel where there are rocks, bars, trees, or other obstructions will divert the streamlines of flow, resulting in a winding path of water within a straight-walled channel. Hence, if one looks closely at a "straight" channel, although the banks of the river may be straight, the flow of water between them is not. However, very few streams even have a straight-walled reach for any distance. A straight course is not the vogue.

The meandering pattern

Since river banks are seldom absolutely straight, when does a stream wind enough to be called meandering? Figure 9.1 shows

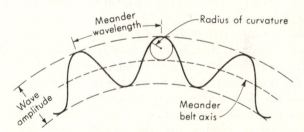

Fig. 9.1 Geometric features of a stream meander. [After Brice (1964).]

a meandering stream and its geometric features. Various ratios have been suggested to describe sinuosity (Table 9.1). There is no complete agreement on an objective criterion for meandering.

The thalweg of a meandering reach is close to the outer side of each bend and crosses over near the point of inflection between the banks. Like the thalweg, streamlines of maximum velocity move downstream, crossing over from one bank to the other (Fig. 9.2).

Table 9.1   Measures of Sinuosity

Sinuosity ratio	Source
$\dfrac{\text{Thalweg length}}{\text{Valley length}}$	Leopold and Wolman (1957)
$\dfrac{\text{Channel length}}{\text{Length of meander belt axis}}$	Brice (1964)
$\dfrac{\text{Stream length}}{\text{Valley length}}$	Schumm (1963)

As the water moves in this winding pattern, it develops a strong centrifugal force which causes a superelevation of the water level on the outside of the bend. Pressure from the excess weight of water piled up in this way intensifies the helical flow at the bend, giving a strong downward movement on the outside, with consequent erosion. The lateral component of velocity shows a movement along the bottom toward the inner part of the bend, where deposition occurs.

On the surface, separation of flow occurs at the inner edge of the bend (Fig. 9.2). At this point there is a backwater eddy with deceleration of flow, hence deposition. Moreover, the separation causes the streamlines of flow to impinge on the outer bank somewhere on the downstream edge of the curve. This offset of the thread of maximum velocity is the reason why point bars grow in a downstream direction and the meander itself moves in the direction of flow.

The profile of a meandering stream shows a series of pools and shallows. The crossover, or point of inflection, of the thread of maximum velocity usually marks a shoal. The deeper sections, or pools, are downstream from the axis of a bend. As already pointed out, the inner sides of bends are areas of deposition, and the outer edges are places of erosion. This combination of erosion and sedimentation at the bends gives a characteristic asymmetric channel cross section as in Fig. 9.2. Pools which exist at the bends are scoured during high flow and are centers of sedimentation at low

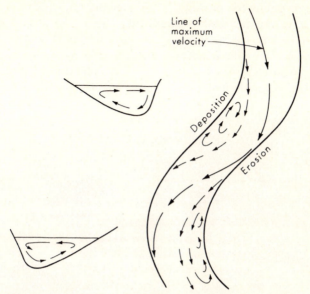

Fig. 9.2 Meandering reach, showing the line of maximum velocity and separation of flow which produce areas of deposition and erosion. Transverse sketches show the lateral movement of water at the bends.

flow. On the other hand, the crossings are scoured at low flow but covered with deposits at high flow.

Causes of meandering

Helical flow is often advanced as the basic cause of meandering. But many other reasons have also been given. One viewpoint is that, when a stream could no longer downcut, it side cut. Along with this went the idea that only mature or old streams meandered. Indeed, meandering was a criterion for these older stages of the stream cycle. However, many streams meander from the time of their origin, even as they are cutting their channels downward.

Shulits adopted Sternberg's theory that gradient is the cause of meandering. These workers felt that slope was a function of the size of grains comprising the bed and that the stream adjusted its slope to the material it must carry. So if the slope exceeds that required to transport the grains on the bed, the stream will meander to lengthen its course and thus decrease the gradient. That is, a stream which falls 5 ft in 3 miles may lengthen its channel by meandering until it takes 5 miles to fall 5 ft.

Plate 18   South Branch of the South Platte River, Colo.

Schumm related sinuosity of rivers on the Great Plains to channel morphology and to size of material in the channel. He found that meandering streams generally had a high amount of silt and clay in their banks and beds. He also discovered that those streams which meandered had deep and narrow channels. Wide, shallow sections of the streams he measured were straighter. In wide, shallow sections, as we have seen in a previous chapter, a large proportion of the total sediment load is carried as bed load. Hence, he suggests that meandering may result when a large proportion of the load is carried as suspended load.

One of the most interesting studies of meandering done in the laboratory was by Friedkin. He tried to create meandering in a number of flume experiments and concluded that sinuosity resulted from local bank erosion and local deposition. Starting with an initially straight channel and with a constant discharge, but with no new material added, he found that the stream would develop meanders. Local erosion of the channel sides initiated the sinuous pattern. This provided a bed load, which was transported a short way and then deposited. He considered that the sediment traveled downstream in a series of intermittent movements from bank to bar to bank. The exchange was over a very short distance, with grains moving along the side of the channel from which they started. On uniform material and slope, he produced a set of uniform bends. The radii of these bends increased when either the discharge or the gradient was increased. Using a variety of material for the channel, he found that in more resistant, fine material the channel was deeper and the gradient more gentle. In coarse material sidewalls were easily eroded, and the channels were wide and shallow, with a steep gradient. Such channels, in coarse material, tended to develop a braided, rather than a meandering, channel pattern.

Once the initial bend was formed, the sinuosity was transmitted downstream, and other bends formed. It seems that the helical flow from the initial curve propagates itself and other bends develop as the water impinges on one bank and is deflected to the other. Friedkin did find that discharge influenced meandering in his experiments and that each discharge seemed to have a meander pattern of its own. The relationship was such that, the larger the discharge, the larger the arc of curvature of the meander.

In actuality, no one explanation fully satisfies as the cause of meandering. Sinuosity probably results from a number of interacting factors, or at one time and under certain conditions meanders arise from one cause, and at another time and under other conditions they occur for a different reason. However, it must certainly be true that the real cause of sinuosity is related to the ability of a stream to adjust to its surroundings.

Meanders and channel morphology

There are definite mathematical relationships between meanders and other aspects of stream morphology. It has been found that the meander wave length and area of the drainage basin are related so that

$$\lambda = aA^b \tag{9.1}$$

where λ is meander wave length, A is basin area, and a and b are empirical constants. And since the discharge of a river is related to its drainage area, discharge and wave length should be related. Friedkin predicted this when he noted the association of discharge and wave length in his flume experiments.

Other relationships which have been established are

$$\lambda = cW^m \tag{9.2}$$

$$A_m = dW^n \tag{9.3}$$

$$\lambda = fR^t \tag{9.4}$$

where λ is wave length, W is channel width, A_m is wave amplitude, R is radius of curvature, and c, d, f, m, n, and t are constants. The exponents in these equations have been found to approximate 1; hence the relationships are almost linear. No doubt there are still other such empirical relationships which could be derived to show the interdependence of the morphological characteristics of meandering streams.

Misfit streams

A misfit stream is one whose meanders do not fit the size of the valley in which the stream is at present flowing. That is, the meanders of the present channel are smaller in amplitude and more intricate than the bends in the valley walls. Misfit streams are widely distributed in certain parts of the world and seem to be regionally developed.

Various theories have been offered to account for the origin of misfit streams. They are said to result from erosion by flood-waters or to be inherited from previous meanders. Some have been ascribed to the influence of rock structure. Still others were formed when the volume of flow of a river was reduced by capture. After intensive study, Dury concluded that most misfit streams are a result of decreased discharge in a changing climate. Using the empirical relationship established for discharge and wave length, he found there was a disparity between the present and past discharges. Past volume of flow was 80 or 100 times the present rate of discharge. This drastic change in runoff could be accounted for during the waning of Pleistocene glaciers. Thus, the former sinuous channel forming the outer valley walls was cut during a period of extremely large flow during recession of the glaciers. Later, when the discharge dwindled because the glaciers were gone, the streams maintained themselves in a much shrunken state on the floors of their former floodplains.

Incised meanders

Incised meanders are formed when the winding channel of a stream is cut deeply into the surface. It has generally been assumed that incision occurs when there is a change in the environment of a river which has been meandering on a floodplain. The change is such that the river renews its downcutting, maintaining the same winding path, which is entrenched in the floodplain. Such meanders are thus inherited from a former cycle of erosion where the stream

Plate 19 Sinuous channel being incised into a floodplain. Near Yellow Springs, Ohio. These become second-cycle incised bends.

had reached maturity or old age before being rejuvenated. However, since a stream may have a sinuous pattern from the beginning of its development, it is possible that some entrenched meanders were formed as the stream cut its original channel. Such first-cycle incised meanders are most likely when a stream of initial low gradient forms on a gently sloping land surface and the region continues to be uplifted as the stream cuts down.

Plate 20 Sinuous channel of the New River, W.Va., which represents original channel incision into the flat-lying rocks of the Appalachian Plateau.

Attempts have been made to establish criteria for determining the origin of incised meanders on a given stream. The most important of these is the transverse profile. If the profile at a bend is asymmetric, with gentler slopes on the inside wall, it is thought to be a first-cycle entrenched meander formed from an initial sinuous pattern. If the cross section at a bend is symmetrical, with steep slopes on both sides of the channel, it is thought that the incised meanders resulted by inheritance from a sinuous pattern of a previous cycle, developed on a floodplain. However, there is no reason to believe that streams are incised vertically; in fact,

Plate 21   Goosenecks of the San Juan River, Utah. These meanders have become deeply incised into the horizontal strata and probably represent first-cycle meanders.

observation proves otherwise. Many streams which are at the present time cutting into their floodplains and entrenching meanders have an asymmetric transverse profile at bends.

Matched, or paired, terraces (Fig. 9.3) are another criterion. The idea here is that if incisement resulted from downcutting on a previous floodplain, uplifted terraces should be found on both sides of a channel. However, again this is rather tenuous evidence. Vigorous side cutting on one side may remove one of the terraces. Or paired terraces may be formed when original downcutting of a sinuous channel takes place on horizontal strata. Thus, neither

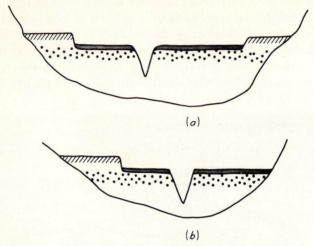

Fig. 9.3 Sketch of terraces, (a) paired and (b) unpaired.

of these criteria is reliable since either may result because of rock type, structure, or side-cutting ability. Whether the incised meanders of a given stream are first- or second-cycle must be determined only after close examination of all factors involved. Unfortunately there is no blanket rule that can be invoked.

The braided pattern

Meandering starts with local bank erosion and then deposition, and perhaps braiding begins in the same way. However, the obvious origin seems to be the appearance of a midchannel bar. This bar grows downstream and may even be built up vertically during highwater stages. The upstream end may become stabilized by the growth of vegetation, which then aids in trapping finer material. Progressive changes take place as the coarse gravel or sandbar becomes a mud flat, then a grass- and willow-covered bar, and then a timbered island, at which point it is considered stabilized. Such a midchannel bar also acts to deflect the current against the sidewalls of the channel, causing erosion.

Plate 22   Channel-bar deposits, above Niagara Falls, N.Y.

A braided stream is characterized by the general instability of the bars and channelways and by caving of the channel walls. Once an initial channel island is formed, the process of division goes on and another bar is formed in one or both of the divided channels. The profile is similar to that of a straight or meandering reach, with pools and shoals.

Causes of braiding

It has been proposed that incompetency is the cause of braiding, that it is only when the bed material is too coarse to be moved that braiding occurs. Accordingly, braiding is the result of the sorting activity of the stream, which moves only those sizes it is competent to handle. However, many investigators have found that debris in the bed and bars of braided rivers are the same size, and thus there seems to be no selective deposition. In some cases, braiding has been attributed to both incompetency and incapacity of a river. That is, the stream can transport neither the amount of debris nor the size of debris that is supplied to it as bed load.

It has generally been found that a braided-channel pattern occurs under conditions of highly variable discharge in rivers with easily erodible banks which can supply an abundant bed load. These factors lead to the necessity for a local high velocity and turbulence

Plate 23   Braided channel of the North Platte River, Nebr.

to enable the stream to do its work. Deposition of the bars is an effective hydraulic device to increase velocity by narrowing the channel. Also, before the bar is built up above water level, deposition serves to decrease the depth of flow, thus increasing roughness and turbulence. Perhaps the real key to the cause of braiding is the proportion of bed load to available discharge.

Braided-channel morphology

Changes in channel morphology and slope occur along with the braiding. Channel width, i.e., the sum of the water surfaces, in a divided reach is greater than the width of the water surface before division. Of course, each divided channel is narrower than the original channel width. Depth of the water in each braided reach is less than the depth of the nonbraided channel. Although effective bottom velocity is greater in a divided reach because of decreased depth, it has been found that, as a result of turbulence, actual forward velocity of flow in naturally braided stretches is less. Moreover, braiding is generally associated with an increase in channel gradient.

Noting that a distinguishing characteristic of braided rivers is the steeper gradient, Leopold and Wolman plotted bank-full discharge against channel slope for a number of natural stream channels (Fig. 9.4). They found that they could draw a line of demarcation such that points representing braided channels lie above it and points representing meandering channels lie below it. Straight channels cannot be distinguished from the graph. With the load factor disregarded, this graph seems to indicate that, for any given discharge, meanders occur at lower slopes than braiding. And for

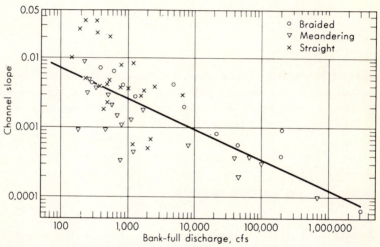

Fig. 9.4 Bank-full discharge plotted against channel gradient for certain braided, meandering, and straight stretches. [After Leopold and Wolman (1957).]

a given slope, meanders will occur at a smaller discharge than will braiding. This might also mean that with a given slope, which the stream for some reason cannot change, an increase in discharge will result in a change from a meandering to a braided habit or that with a given discharge, if a stream increases its gradient, it will also change its pattern from a meandering to a braided one. However, it must be borne in mind that amount and caliber of bed load supplied to the river, in relation to the discharge, also seem to be important factors.

Channel pattern and grade

It seems, then, that the map plan is part of the overall adjustment of a stream and also represents an adaptation of a river to environmental controls. The channel pattern varies with amount and caliber of load and with change in discharge. It also varies as a result of the interaction, within the steady state, of changes in channel morphology. We could then amend Eq. (8.9) to read

$$nSFP = \frac{kL^a D^b}{Q^c} \qquad (9.5)$$

where P is channel pattern. Thus, like the cross section and longitudinal profile, the channel pattern, whether straight, sinuous, or braided, is determined by the simultaneous response of a river to the discharge and load provided to it.

REFERENCES AND SELECTED READINGS

Bagnold, R. A. (1960)   Some aspects of the shape of river meanders: U.S. Geol. Surv. Prof. Paper 282E.

Brice, J. C. (1964)   Channel patterns and terraces of the Loup Rivers in Nebraska: U.S. Geol. Surv. Prof. Paper 422D.

Dury, G. H. (1960)   Misfit streams: problems in interpretation, discharge and distribution: Geograph. Rev., vol. 50, no. 2, pp. 219–242.

Eakin, H. M. (1935)   Diversity of current direction and load distribution on stream-bends: Trans. Am. Geophys. Union, pt. 2, pp. 467–472.

Fahnestock, R. K. (1963)   Morphology and hydrology of a glacial stream, White River, Mt. Rainier, Wash.: U.S. Geol. Surv. Prof. Paper 422A.

Friedkin, J. F. (1945)   A laboratory study of the meandering of alluvial rivers: U.S. Waterways Experiment Station.

Leopold, L. B., and M. G. Wolman (1957)   River channel patterns—braided, meandering, straight: U.S. Geol. Surv. Prof. Paper 282B.

Matthes, G. H. (1941)   Basic aspects of stream meanders: Trans. Am. Geophys. Union, vol. 22, pp. 632–636.

Schumm, S. A. (1963)   Sinuosity of alluvial rivers of the Great Plains: Geol. Soc. Am. Bull., vol. 74, pp. 1089–1100.

Shulits, S. (1941)   Rational equation of river bed profiles: Trans. Am. Geophys. Union, vol. 22, pp. 622–629.

Werner, P. W. (1951)   On the origin of river meanders: Trans. Am. Geophys. Union, vol. 32, pp. 898–902.

10

The river basin

The geomorphologist is interested, not only in
a stream itself, but also in the morphological
unit of a stream which is its drainage basin.
A river basin represents the area drained by a
stream and its tributaries. It is bounded by a
divide, which separates it from adjacent watersheds.

For purposes of comparison within and
among drainage areas, a hierarchy of streams
has been set up wherein streams are ranked
according to order. Although other methods of
stream ordering have been suggested, that
proposed by Strahler is more objective and
straightforward. According to his system,
fingertip tributaries at the head of a stream
system are designated as first-order streams.
Two first-order streams join to form a second-
order stream segment; two second-order
streams join, forming a third-order, and so
on (Fig. 10.1). It takes at least two streams
of any given order to form a stream of the

next higher order. However, a given order may have more than two lower-order segments: for example, a third-order stream may have 9 first-order tributaries (it has to have at least 4) and 3 second-orders (it has to have at least 2). The main branch of the river is always the highest order of the basin. The watershed in Fig. 10.1 is a fourth-order basin.

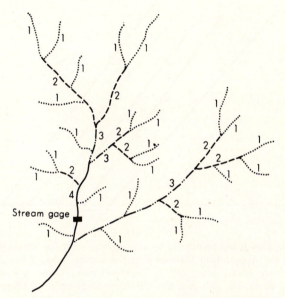

Fig. 10.1 Hierarchy of stream ordering. Numbers and pattern indicate order of respective segments. The watershed is fourth-order.

Laws of drainage composition

Horton and others have proposed that there is an orderly development of drainage basins according to a group of "laws" of drainage composition. Horton noted that the number of streams of different orders in a watershed decreases with increasing order in a regular way. In fact, when the logarithms of the number of streams of a given order are plotted against the order, the points lie on a straight line (Fig. 10.2). The regression equation for this line is given in Table 10.1. The slope of the linear regression line, R_b, is the same as the bifurcation ratio, i.e, the ratio of the number

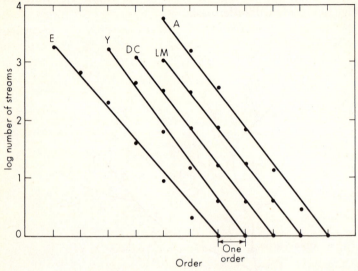

Fig. 10.2   Plot of log number of streams against order for certain drainage basins in the Appalachian Plateau. *E* is the Emory River, Tenn., *Y* is the Youghiogheny River, Md., *DC* is Daddys Creek, Tenn., *LM* is Little Mahoning River, Pa., and *A* is the Allegheny River in N.Y. [Adapted from Morisawa (1962).]

of streams of one order to the number of streams of the next higher order. The relationship shown by the graph (Fig. 10.1) and the regression equation has been called the *law of stream numbers*. The same kind of relationship seems to exist between order of streams and their lengths, order and areas, order and gradients, and order and relief of the basin (Table 10.1). Many watersheds have been shown to conform to these laws as set forth.

However, although most basins do tend to conform to the laws of drainage composition, there are exceptions. Noting that many stream networks do not conform strictly to Horton's law of stream numbers, Shreve has suggested that the law simply represents a statistical relationship. That is, rather than denoting an orderly development of drainage systems, the law of stream numbers results from the random growth of drainage basins. Also, in some watersheds higher-order stream segments are shorter than they should be if the law of stream lengths is valid. It may be that, in this case, lack of agreement with the law is a result of the Strahler method of ordering. Horton considered the length of a higher-order stream to extend from the head in a fingertip tributary to its mouth, whereas the Strahler method breaks a stream up into segments. This makes higher-order segments shorter than those from which Horton derived his law.

Table 10.1   Laws of Drainage Composition

Law	Mathematical expression*	Source
Stream numbers	$N_u = R_b{}^{s-u}$	Horton (1945)
Stream lengths	$\bar{L}_u = \bar{L}_1 R_L{}^{u-1}$	Horton (1945)
Basin areas	$\bar{A}_u = \bar{A}_1 R_a{}^{u-1}$	Horton (1945), Schumm (1956)
Stream gradients	$\bar{S}_u = \bar{S}_1 R_s{}^{s-u}$	Horton (1945), Morisawa (1962)
Basin relief	$\bar{H}_u = \bar{H}_1 R_R{}^{u-1}$	Morisawa (1962)

* Symbols are as follows:

R_b = bifurcation ratio, ratio of number of streams of a given order u to number of streams of next higher order

N_u = number of streams of a given order u

s = highest order of stream in a given basin

$\bar{L}_u$ = average length of streams of order u

$\bar{A}_u$ = average area of basins of order u

$\bar{S}_u$ = average slope of streams of order u

$\bar{H}_u$ = average relief of basins of order u

R_L = stream-length ratio

R_a = area ratio

R_s = gradient ratio, or slope ratio

R_R = basin-relief ratio

The laws of basin areas and relief seem to be valid for the data accumulated thus far. However, all basins do not conform to the law of stream gradients. For example, in some watersheds of the Appalachian Plateau, the curve of the logarithm of stream gradient against order is not a straight line. Deviations from the straight line postulated may result from variation in lithology of the rocks through which the stream is cutting or from regional uplift. If a river basin in a region of horizontal strata has its finger-tip tributaries flowing on a resistant layer, these lower-order streams will have a gradient less than that of the higher orders which are flowing on less resistant rock. Also, an uplift or relative lowering of base level will cause the streams to lower their gradients by scour. This degradation will start at the mouth and move progressively upstream. Lower-order segments, being the last to regrade their channels, will thus tend to have lower gradients than they should according to the law of stream gradients. All these inconsistencies, along with Shreve's work, indicate that more investigations of the laws of drainage composition are needed before we can affirm or deny that they are laws.

Constant of channel maintenance

That there really is an orderly extension of a drainage system seems to be shown by a study of the relationship between basin areas and channel lengths (Fig. 10.3). In particular, average basin area

$$\bar{A}_u$$

and total stream length

$$\sum_{u=1}^{u} L_u$$

are related by a linear equation

$$\bar{A}_u = a + C \sum_{u=1}^{u} L_u \tag{10.1}$$

The slope of this linear regression, C, is called the *constant of channel maintenance* and represents the area in square feet necessary to develop and maintain 1 ft of drainage channel. It is therefore the lower limiting area required for expansion of a drainage system in a given region. A watershed surfaced with an impervious and impermeable silt requires a smaller drainage area to maintain

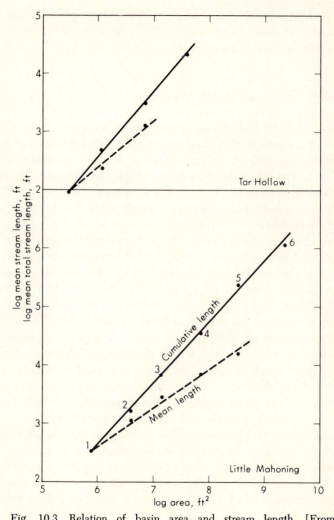

Fig. 10.3 Relation of basin area and stream length. [From Morisawa (1959).]

a permanent channel than does a watershed on porous sand. The constant of channel maintenance is thus a measure of the erodibility of the land surface of a watershed.

Drainage density and stream frequency

Drainage density and stream frequency are measures of the dissection of a watershed. Drainage density is length of stream channel per unit area. Stream frequency is the number of channels per unit area. Drainage density seems to be independent of order, but channel density has been found to decrease with order. These conclusions are tentative, for not enough work has been done to verify the trends.

Both drainage density and stream frequency depend upon the climate and physical characteristics of the watershed. Climate exerts an important influence directly by determining discharge, as well as indirectly by its effects on vegetation. Rock and soil types are important factors, since they determine the resistance of the surface to erosion. In general, a basin underlain by clay or shale has a high drainage density and stream frequency. A watershed underlain by sandstone has a low channel and drainage density. In a region which is rugged or has great relief, if other factors are the same, drainage density and channel frequency are high. In analyzing any given watershed, the influence of all these factors has to be weighed and balanced, one against the other.

It should also be pointed out that drainage density is the reciprocal of the constant of channel maintenance; hence a basin with low drainage density has a high constant of channel maintenance. In other words, if it requires a large drainage area to maintain 1 ft of stream channel, the length of channel per unit area must be small.

Basin shape

A number of methods have been proposed to describe basin shape in quantitative terms (Table 10.2). In considering shape, one must

Table 10.2 **Some Proposed Basin-shape Measures**

Shape factor	Definition	Source
Form F	$\dfrac{\text{Basin area}}{(\text{Basin length})^2}$	Horton (1932)
Shape S	$\dfrac{(\text{Basin length})^2}{\text{Basin area}}$	Corps of Engineers
Shape S	$\dfrac{\text{Basin length}}{\text{Basin width}}$	Horton (1932)
Circularity ratio C	$\dfrac{\text{Basin area}}{\text{Area of a circle with same basin perimeter}}$	Miller (1953)
Elongation ratio E	$\dfrac{\text{Diameter of circle of basin area}}{\text{Maximum length of basin}}$	Schumm (1956)
Lemniscate ratio k	$\dfrac{(\text{Basin length})^2}{4(\text{basin area})}$	Chorley et al. (1957)

remember that extreme irregularity along a divide may exert a control on the length of the perimeter, changing it more than it does the area involved. Evaluation of these various measures of shape depends on their usefulness and applicability. Circularity and elongation ratio may be of practical use in predicting certain hydrologic characteristics of a drainage basin. And elongation ratio has also been used in studies of sediment loss in watersheds.

How does a basin shape change with order and with increasing size of drainage area? In regions of homogeneous rock and structure one might think larger basins should be more circular. Data which have been gathered so far seem to indicate that shape of drainage basins is independent of order or size. Much more study needs to be done on the form of drainage basins.

Interrelationship of basin characteristics

Since, by the laws of drainage composition, number of streams, stream lengths, gradients, basin areas, and basin relief are all related to order, they should be related mathematically to each other. We have already seen how the constant of channel maintenance was derived from the relationship of total stream length to basin area. Various investigators have found that, in very diverse regions, basin area and longest length from head to mouth of a stream were related by an equation

$$L = kA^n \qquad (10.2)$$

Similar relationships of other basin characteristics have been shown to hold true, relating length, gradient, relief, and area to each other. Some of these have already been mentioned. Such kinds of interrelationships among the morphometric properties of watersheds on the Appalachian Plateau are shown in Table 10.3. These and other correlations that have been established show that large basins tend to have longer streams with gentler gradients and fewer first-order tributaries and that watersheds with steep valley-wall slopes have a fine texture, high relief, and streams with steep gradients.

Table 10.3 Interrelationships of Basin Characteristics, Appalachian Plateau

Basin area A*	Total stream length ΣL	Circularity C
$\Sigma L = a_1 A^n$	$\dfrac{1}{S} = b_1 \Sigma L^h$	$F_1 = c_1 C^g$
$\dfrac{1}{S} = a_2 A^m$	$\dfrac{1}{C} = b_2 \Sigma L^j$	$R = c_2 C^d$
$\dfrac{1}{C} = a_3 A^r$	$\dfrac{1}{R} = b_3 \Sigma L^k$	
$\dfrac{1}{R} = a_4 A^s$	$\dfrac{1}{F_1} = b_4 \Sigma L^l$	
$\dfrac{1}{F_1} = a_5 A^t$		

* S is stream gradient, R is relief ratio, and F_1 is first-order stream frequency.

Effects of lithology

The influence of rock structure and lithology has been emphasized previously in discussing the morphometric characteristics of stream channels. Lithology and rock structure also have important effects on the morphometry and geometry of drainage basins. A flat-lying, resistant bed will cause an increase in stream length and in drainage area and a decrease in stream gradient. However, in areas where sediments are folded, streams cutting across resistant strata will be short and steep, with small drainage areas.

Streams flowing on coarse-grained sediment have been found to be much longer than streams of the same order on fine-grained sediment, their basins are much larger, and their drainage densities much less. In an area of unconsolidated beach and lake-bed materials, it was determined that streams on sandy layers are straighter and their channel patterns simpler than those formed on silt. Stream

lengths and drainage-basin areas on dolomite are greater than those
of comparable order on sandstone or shale.

Lithology and drainage pattern

The effects of lithology and rock structure are most evident in
the drainage patterns of well-developed drainage basins (Fig.
10.4). On an absolutely flat surface of homogeneous rock, a drain-

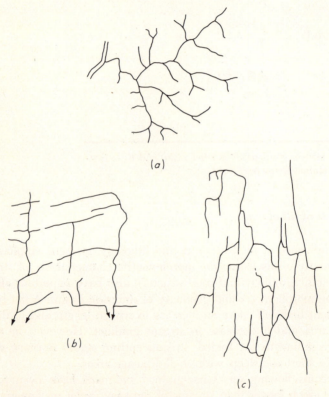

Fig. 10.4 Types of drainage patterns. (*a*) A dendritic pattern
developed on homogeneous, flat-lying strata. From the Charleston,
W.Va., quadrangle. (*b*) Rectangular drainage pattern developed
on jointed rock. From the Kingston West, N.Y., quadrangle. (*c*)
Trellised pattern developed on folded strata. From the Kaaterskill,
N.Y., quadrangle. (Drainage patterns are drawn to different
scales.)

age net should form at random, with the possibility of streamflow equal in all directions, giving what is termed a *dendritic drainage pattern.* Actually, both absolutely flat and absolutely homogeneous surfaces are rare in nature so that real-life distributions of flow directions should be expected to vary from the ideal. Local ground slope and local variation in geology exert an influence on flow direction and drainage-pattern development.

The influence of surface slope is shown by the development of parallel rills, gullies, or channels on steep surface slopes of road cuts, hillsides, and broad-channel side slopes. For the same reason, radial drainage patterns are developed on domes or volcanic cones.

The influence of rock resistance and structure is shown by the development of drainage patterns on jointed or folded rocks. Here the streams find it easier to erode a channel along a weakness. If joints are the weakness, their orientation determines the stream pattern (Fig. 10.4*b*). In a similar way, streams develop along linear bands of outcropping weak rock in tilted or folded strata. While some original (consequent) rivers may maintain their courses across more resistant rocks, in general tributaries find it easier to erode channels in the weaker beds. This gives rise to a trellised

Plate 24   Stream erosion along joints in the Keyserkill, N.Y. (Courtesy of G. Dougherty.)

drainage pattern (Fig. 10.4*c*). Thus, streams always seek out and take advantage of any weakness in the rocks over which they flow.

Growth and steady state of drainage basins

The development of a drainage network proceeds by the concentration of runoff and the deepening and widening of initial rills to gullies, which are permanent channels. Those gullies which have a favored position, because they collect more runoff and/or because they are floored by weaker material, grow laterally at the expense of neighboring channels. When the lateral and vertical growth of the gully provides enough of a surface, tributary rills develop on the sidewalls, elaborating the drainage net. At the same time, headward erosion results in either the elongation of a stream or its bifurcation into two branches (Fig. 10.5). The important limiting elements in drainage development, as far as elaboration and elongation are concerned, are the constant of channel maintenance and available relief. Extension of the network can occur only if there is an area, equal to or larger than the constant of channel maintenance, still available. And only while there is enough relief can headward erosion take place.

However, even while tributaries are being extended and elaboration is taking place, integration of the net is proceeding. Some channels are lost by abstraction and absorption. Abstraction occurs when a more aggressive stream expands to take over its neighbor, i.e., by the elimination of one stream by another, which captures its channel and drainage area. A tributary is lost by absorption when the water table falls below its channel and it can thus no longer flow. These processes of simplification and integration of the drainage net are shown in Fig. 10.5.

Thus, within the same drainage basin, tributaries are being added in some places and lost in others, and some stream segments are being lengthened and other streams are being shortened. Thus, over the whole basin, gain and loss are balanced. Adjustments in the watershed system are tending toward the establishment and maintenance of an equilibrium. The equilibrium is a dynamic one, since the network and morphologic characteristics of the basin

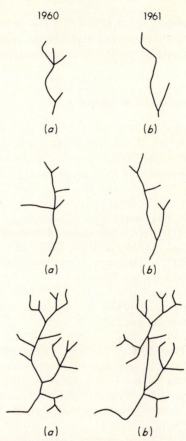

Fig. 10.5 Changes in drainage nets of some developing watersheds, Hebgen Lake, Mont. [After Morisawa (1964).]

are constantly changing. So it seems that just as each stream within a drainage basin tends toward an equilibrium condition, or "grade," so the whole watershed itself seeks to establish a steady state.

REFERENCES AND SELECTED READINGS

Carlston, C. W. (1966) The effect of climate on drainage density and streamflow; Intern. Assoc. Hydrol. XI Année, no. 3, pp. 62–69.

Chorley, R. S., D. E. G. Malm, and H. A. Pogorzelski (1957) A new standard for estimating basin shape: Am. Jour. Sci., vol. 255, pp. 138–141.

Glock, W. S. (1931) The development of drainage systems: a synoptic review; Geograph. Rev., vol. 21, pp. 475–482.

Gray, D. M. (1961) Interrelationships of watershed characteristics: Jour. Geophys. Res., vol. 66, no. 4, pp. 1215–1223.

Horton, R. E. (1932) Drainage basin characteristics: Trans. Am. Geophys. Union, vol. 13, pp. 350–361.

——— (1945) Erosional development of streams and their drainage basins: hydrophysical approach to quantitative morphology: Geol. Soc. Am. Bull., vol. 56, pp. 275–370.

Langbein, W., and others (1947) Topographic characteristics of drainage basins: U.S. Geol. Surv. Water Supply Paper 968C.

Miller, V. C. (1953) A quantitative geomorphic study of drainage basin characteristics in the Clinch Mt. area: Va. and Tenn.: Tech. Rept. 3, Office Naval Res. Proj. NR 389-042, Columbia University.

Morisawa, M. E. (1958) Measurement of drainage basin outline form: Jour. Geol., vol. 66, pp. 587–591.

——— (1962) Quantitative geomorphology of some watersheds in the Appalachian Plateau: Geol. Soc. Am. Bull., vol. 73, pp. 1025–1046.

Schenck, H., Jr. (1963) Simulation of the evolution of drainage-basin networks with a digital computer: Jour. Geophys. Res., vol. 68, pp. 5739–5745.

Schumm, S. A. (1956) Evolution of drainage systems and slopes in badlands at Perth Amboy, N.J.: Geol. Soc. Am. Bull., vol. 67, pp. 597–646.

Shreve, R. L. (1966) Statistical law of stream numbers: Jour. Geol., vol. 74, pp. 17–37.

Strahler, A. N. (1957) Quantitative analysis of watershed geomorphology: Trans. Am. Geophys. Union, vol. 38, pp. 913–920.

Name Index

Adams, F. D., 5, 9
Agricola, 4
Anderson, A. G., 63, 64
Aristotle, 2–4
Avicenna, 4

Bagnold, R. A., 150
Baulig, H., 118
Benedict, P. C., 46
Bernoulli, D., 8, 67
Blissenbach, E., 97
Borland, W. M., 65
Boussinesq, J., 8
Brice, J. C., 132, 133, 137, 138, 150
Brooks, N. H., 60, 61, 64, 65, 111, 118
Brush, L. M., Jr., 49, 65, 105, 108, 112, 118
Buckley, A. B., 8
Bull, W. B., 94, 95, 97

Carlston, C. W., 166
Chorley, R. J., 133, 159, 166
Chow, Ven Te, 38, 40, 64
Colby, B. R., 64, 97, 116, 118

Corbett, D. M., 27
Crickmay, C. H., 108, 118
Culling, W. E. H., 125, 129, 133

Dalrymple, T., 26, 27
Daussé, M. F. B., 7
da Vinci, Leonardo, 3
Davis, W. M., 6, 7, 9, 122, 123, 125
de Chézy, A. L., 8
Dempster, G. R., Jr., 65
DeSaussure, H. B., 5
Desmarest, N., 5
Dole, R. B., 42, 66, 79
Douglas, I., 64
DuBoys, P., 8
Dury, J. H., 143, 150

Eakin, H. M., 150
Einstein, H. A., 63, 64
Eisenlohr, W. S., Jr., 24, 27
Euler, L., 8

Fahnestock, R. K., 150
Fisk, H. N., 89–91, 97

167

Subject Index

Abrasion (*see* Corrasion)
Absorption of tributaries, 164
Abstraction of tributaries, 164
Aggradation (*see* Deposition)
Allegheny River, hydrograph of, 23
  rating curve for, 22
  storm hydrograph of, 24
Alluvial fan, 94–96
Amazon River, 1, 2
Antidunes, 57, 58, 60

Bahada, 96
Base level, 122
Bed configuration, 55–59
Bed load, Boise River, 46
  definition, 46, 55
  measurement of, 46
  movement, 47
  transport, 55–59
Bifurcation ratio, 155
Boundary layer, 32
  and particle size, 33
Braided channel, 146–149
  causes, 147, 148
  definition, 80, 135
  morphology, 148, 149

Braiding (*see* Braided channel)

Capacity, 123, 132
  definition, 53
  factors determining, 54, 55
  loss of, 81
Catastrophism, 4
Cavitation, 67–69
Channel, bed configuration, 33, 56–58
  development, 70, 71
  erosion, 4
  length (*see* Stream length)
  morphometry, 29
  pattern, 135–151
    and grade, 150
  shape, 110–117
    and lithology, 112, 113
  stable, 124, 126, 127, 129, 130
  widening, 71, 72
Channel maintenance, constant of, 156
Chemical erosion (*see* Corrosion)
Chézy formula, 37, 110
Circularity ratio, 159–160
Climate and basin hydrology, 20
Colorado River, area, 14
  canyon, 6, 72